Additional Praise for
Psychic Abilities for Beginners

"Melanie demonstrates simple but effective ways to show you how to tap into your own intuition with clarity and confidence that will surely help you accept your own psychic gift(s)."

—Kristy Robinett, author of
Messenger Between Worlds

"Barnum's book covers a diverse range of psychic abilities ... [it's] a treat to read and an essential for the developing psychic's reference shelf."

—Alexandra Chauran, author of
Clairvoyance for Beginners

"Packed with useful information and really fascinating anecdotes. I recommend *Psychic Abilities for Beginners* for anyone wanting to step into their authentic self."

—Dr. Tammy Nelson, author of
What's Eating You?

"You'll be riveted to the page when reading Melanie Barnum's new book."

—Melissa Alvarez, author of
Your Psychic Self

Psychic Abilities
for Beginners

© Alicia Craybas

About the Author

Melanie Barnum (Bethel, CT) is a psychic medium, intuitive counselor, life coach, and hypnotist who has been practicing professionally for more than fifteen years. She was a VIP Reader at Psych Out, a gathering of the nation's foremost psychics, organized by Court TV. Barnum is also an Angelspeake Facilitator, a Remote Viewer, and a member of the National Guild of Hypnotists (NGH) and the International Association of Counselors and Therapists (IACT). Visit her online at MelanieBarnum.com.

Psychic Abilities

For Beginners

Awaken Your Intuitive Senses

Melanie Barnum

Llewellyn Publications
Woodbury, Minnesota

FIRST EDITION
Fifth Printing, 2017

Cover art: www.iStockpho.com/22772377/© lg0rZh
Cover design by Lisa Novak
Edited by Stephanie Finne
Interior art by the Llewellyn Art Department

Llewellyn Publications is a registered trademark of Llewellyn Worldwide Ltd.

Library of Congress Cataloging-in-Publication Data
Barnum, Melanie, 1969–
  Psychic abilities for beginners : awaken your intuitive senses / by
Melanie Barnum. — First Edition.
     pages cm
  Includes bibliographical references.
  ISBN 978-0-7387-4183-3
1. Parapsychology. 2. Psychic ability. 3. Intuition—Miscellanea. I.
Title.
  BF1031.B26 2014
  133.8—dc23
                              2014016185

Llewellyn Publications
A Division of Llewellyn Worldwide Ltd.
2143 Wooddale Drive
Woodbury, MN 55125-2989
www.llewellyn.com

Printed in the United States of America

Other Books by Melanie Barnum

The Book of Psychic Symbols

The Steady Way to Greatness

Dedication

This book is dedicated to my family, who've stuck by me, encouraging me, loving me. Tom, you are my rock, both physically and mentally, and I'm glad you listened to your intuition and didn't take no for an answer. Molly, my Molly Bug, you shine more than you can imagine as you are beautiful inside and out! And Samantha, my Nugget, you are blossoming and in the beginnings of a life filled with love and laughter. Together you are all the most incredible people I know!

Acknowledgments

Writing this, my third book, has been exciting and challenging! At times my fingers flew over the keyboard and other times I couldn't put a sentence together to save my life. I thank every other author who has come before me, experiencing the same ebbs and flows, but who persevered in order to get their words to the people who needed it. My sincere hope is that I've done the same—delivered the messages to the people who need and desire to read them in a way we can all understand.

I've had incredible teachers along the way. I consider these people to be not only mentors but also friends to whom I'm grateful, and the entire Llewellyn family—especially Angela Wix, a brilliant, kind, and patient editor, and Brett Fechheimer, who reads my drivel and helps me to make it better.

I know my mom, my best friend, is looking down, smiling—happy to help me meet my deadlines and pursue my desires that were once only wild fantasies. My radiant sister, Tammy, and her entire family have encouraged, questioned, and even chastised me when necessary during my writing process. And my brother, because I know somewhere he is rooting me on. For that, I am more than appreciative.

And, to my friends who understood my withdrawal into the writing zone and have encouraged me with cookies; I thank you, even if my waistline doesn't. And, Heather, one of these days you will believe. ;-)

Lastly, again, I would be nothing without my family. The books I've written and the successes I've had with my clients would mean absolutely nothing without the love and never-ending support I've felt from my incredible husband, Tom, and my two beautiful, kind, intelligent daughters, light workers in their own right, Molly and Samantha.

Above all, thank you, the readers, for continuing to enjoy and share my books. Not only am I able to impart the wisdom and exercises I've included in these pages, but you, the intuitive beings, are also helping me to grow and experience life in a whole new way!

Thanks to all and enjoy!

"The only real valuable thing is intuition."

—ALBERT EINSTEIN

contents

exercises

Editor's Note

The practices and techniques described in this book should not be used as an alternative to professional medical treatment. This book does not attempt to give medical diagnosis, treatment, prescriptions, or suggestions for medication in relation to any human disease, pain, injury, deformity, or physical or mental condition.

The author and publisher of this book are not responsible in any manner whatsoever for any injury that may occur through following the examples contained herein. It is recommended that you consult your physician to obtain a diagnosis for any physical or mental symptoms you may experience.

introduction

"Psychic ability is part of everyone's birthright."
—WILLIAM W. HEWITT

Reality

What do you mean?" my client Sara asked me during a reading about five years ago.

"Well, I have an image in my mind's eye of you walking down the aisle with a wedding dress on, and I'm hearing 'forty,'" I responded, knowing she wasn't going to much care for the answer to her question. She'd asked when she would meet the man she would marry.

"Hmmm. That doesn't make sense to me. I'm only thirty-six now. Maybe he's forty," she replied, hoping this was true.

"Maybe. But I'm hearing forty. Don't worry, it'll be worth the wait!" I exclaimed. "I can also tell you that you will meet him through mutual friends and it has something to do with bicycles."

"Okay, but I'm going to assume it's he who will be forty. I am not planning on waiting that long!" she insisted.

Five years later, she's back in my office.

"So, guess what? You're never going to believe it," she laughed.

"Oh, I think I will believe it," I chuckled back.

Sara, now forty, tells me she is about to walk down the aisle, having met the man she is marrying when she walked into a bicycle store. Mutual friends introduced them. I had seen and heard her wedding intuitively, using my psychic senses. I can honestly say, even though I've been practicing for almost two decades, it still amazes and fascinates me each time I get a psychic hit so accurately.

Everyone, that's right, *everyone* has some type of natural intuitive sense. For some, it's stronger and comes with a desire to develop it. If you've picked up this book, you have that desire, or at the very least you are curious about how your psychic senses work. From curiosity stems knowledge and the hope that there is more out there. Hope is what keeps us going, what motivates us to continue. Hope that we will be happy. Tuning in to your psychic senses will help give you hope that a wonderful existence is yours for the taking.

We are all intuitive beings. Believing in our abilities is the first step toward living an extraordinary life and being privy to all the guidance the universe has to offer. "When we embrace our psychic potential, we embrace our soul's potential—the potential to use our innate ability to connect with the natural forces that lie beyond the material world, beyond the five senses." (Chestney, 2004) Our psychic senses are not physical, they are spiritual. Once we've accepted that, we can hold the keys to the universe.

In the Beginning

Many, many years ago it felt like I was hit over the head, and I heard the words, "You have to do this work now." Being a logical and rational person, I was never going to just start advertising as a "psychic," so I set out to learn everything I could about my intuitive abilities. I began taking classes and offering free psychic readings so I could sharpen my instincts. Along the way, I learned what psychic senses were and how they present in real life for me and for others. As the late humanitarian writer Maya Angelou said, "All great achievements require time." I spent many years practicing until I felt comfortable and proficient enough to offer sessions professionally.

I never realized, though I knew I could always read people, that what I did was any different from what anyone else did. I didn't know that most people didn't see spirits such as Henry, our family ghost, passing by me down the stairs as I scaled the molding above like a monkey. This, I recently found out, really did happen to my sister as well. Other than that particularly nonchalant ghost, I was pretty normal.

I am a psychic and a medium (yes, I talk to dead people). I read my clients' energy to glean information about their past, their present, and their future. I enjoy seeing the light in someone's eyes when I connect to their loved ones on the other side. Even more exciting is when their dead relatives assemble together and come through in full force. What I love even more is the *aha* moment—that second when I've said something I have no possible way of knowing that means so much to my sitter that I have to figuratively help them pick their jaw up off the floor. It is in that exact instant when they are truly open to receiving messages.

I have been lucky; I've been able to tap into my greatness, the energy that connects me to others. That very prolific message I heard—"You need to do this work now"—changed the direction my life was headed. That psychic bat to my head jump-started my career and created a turning point that helped me bring comfort and direction to others as well. Along with reading for my psychic clients over the phone and out of my Ridgefield, Connecticut, office, I teach regularly, mentor others, hold gallery events, and am certified in hypnotism, reflexology, Reiki, and hypno/life coaching.

I am a professional psychic, not just because I developed my abilities, but because I was able to recognize my innate gifts. I slowly began to comprehend that by raising my own vibrational frequency I connected to the energy of the universe, which allowed me to begin utilizing this psychic knowledge. We all have the capacity to extend our vibration upward, toward our own highest personal frequency. The greater we expand upon this energy, the more we will connect to the other side or our ESP (see this chapter's Where It All Began section).

My client Barbara was in yesterday for a session. We were discussing destiny and karma and our beliefs in those areas. We talked about our choices and how they affect us and how karma is not just negative but positive as well (see chapter 12). This led to a conversation about extrasensory abilities and whether we are each predestined to be either psychic or not. While I believe we can reach our full potential in all things, I explained to her that even though not all of us will excel, we all have natural intuition and we need to trust in the feelings we get. There is a difference between knowing and acknowledging the psychic path is there and walking down that psychic path. That's a choice.

Not everyone will decide to become a professional psychic intuitive. Actually, most people won't. But all of you—and all people—have the ability to develop, for your own well-being, your intuitive gifts. Becoming acquainted with your talents will open up a whole new understanding of the world and those who live in it. Once you are comfortable with this new energy, feeling at home with this increased level of receptivity, it is easier to exist in this extraordinary state of awareness. The benefits of tapping into this incredible vibrational frequency are immense: a greater understanding of who you are, an increase in pure, unadulterated joy, an obtainment of powerful wisdom and insights previously overlooked, and so much more. With practice, you will discover the most important thing—who you truly are.

Believing psychic ability is genuine is the first step on your journey to spiritual development. I always encourage people to gain their own understanding of intuition rather than trying to prove to them that it's real. Shutting your eyes to the possibilities only shuts down your personal intuition; it doesn't prove that it's nonexistent. Opening to your potential will be proof enough that psychic powers exist.

I am a skeptic, a healthy skeptic, but one nonetheless. Being a skeptic does not mean I'm a nonbeliever. It simply means I don't believe all events have a paranormal connection. Sometimes the toy in the room started talking simply because the batteries surged, or the dog was barking while looking to the top of the stairs because he watched a bug fly up. There is not always a mystical reason for everything.

However, I also know that psychic ability is authentic. I've experienced it. I've had numerous e-mails, phone calls, and messages from clients saying what I've predicted has come to pass or what I'd told them during their reading that they were unable to validate in that moment was proved to them within days of their session with me. I've been connected to my clients' deceased loved ones who have come through with evidence, things that I never could have known, including names, dates, events, etc., to provide guidance or to simply extend messages of love and encouragement. All of these occurrences were made possible through the use of my psychic senses.

Where It All Began

Extrasensory perception, or ESP, has been around since the beginning of time, though it was not always recognized as such. The old sages, priests, oracles, and trusted advisers of kings and leaders were said to have prophesied many events for their rulers. From when to plant the crops to whether or not to go to war and everything in between, these mostly trusted psychics were consulted on a regular basis.

Nostradamus is one of the more modern and famous psychics. He predicted more than 6,300 events; mostly natural disasters, murders, and wars. Though he didn't date them, believers and scholars are able to relate most of his prophecies since his death in 1566 to actual events throughout history up to modern times, although some claim there are numerous interpretations to be made, which of course there are.

Edgar Cayce, hailed as the father of holistic medicine, was known as the "sleeping prophet" and had been a psychic since childhood. He communicated with his late grandfather and played with "imaginary" friends. As he grew older, he began to use trance as his mode of receiving psychic information. He would lie down on the couch, close his eyes, fold his arms over his abdomen, and meditate, hence the "sleeping prophet" moniker. While his readings for others focused mainly on holistic health and diagnosing and often healing illness or disease, his sessions included numerous insights about ancient history and the alterations of land, many of which have now been proven to be true. He devoted his life to studying and teaching others about ESP, spiritual growth, philosophy, dreams, the Akashic Records, reincarnation, and more. There are hundreds of books written about him and his readings. In 1931, before his death in 1945, Cayce began the Association for Research and Enlightenment (A.R.E.) in Virginia. It is there you will gain access to more than fourteen thousand of his actual readings.

Exercise: Where It Began for You

Get yourself a journal or a notebook to use for the many exercises to come in this book. This way you can record everything you work on and keep it to refer back to. You can also repeat the exercises and compare how far you've come!

This first exercise is simple. As I said, intuition and psychic senses have been present for as long as we've been around, but for us, as individuals, there is usually an *aha* moment or that time when you were truly curious about what just happened or how you could've known something. That was your beginning—that time when you became aware that there was more to life than what you could understand with your physical senses.

This moment in your life is very important because it was your opening. It doesn't mean that you will remember it perfectly, or that you instantly became psychic. It just means you became aware of the possibilities. Write down this moment. Include where you were, who you were with, what you were doing, and what the moment was about. Describe it with as much detail as possible.

You may find that you have to record a more recent memory or event because you can't seem to recall the first, initial, sensitizing event. That's okay. You can go back and write down another, earlier one if it comes to you; and then, you can do it again! There is no wrong answer; it's about your own personal awareness.

We Are All Intuitive

While not every psychic will become as famously known as Nostradamus or Edgar Cayce and not every intuitive will become a renowned psychic, every person does use their intuition on a daily basis. We use it when we have a visceral or gut reaction to something, when we feel we've already met the person we've just been introduced to, when we buy milk at the store simply because of an urge though when we left we thought we had plenty, and when we just know something but have no idea how we know it. We are all intuitive in some way.

I teach people to develop their own intuition. One of the most difficult roadblocks for most people to get past is determining whether the information they are seeing, hearing, feeling, or believing is real or an illusion. This, of course, makes perfect sense! Discernment is hard, even for professionals like me who have been doing this for a long time. I tell people all the time, "If you don't feel like you're getting anything psychically, imagine you are!" This is not because you should "fake it till you make it"; I'm not asking anyone to be phony. You need to believe in your intuition enough to acknowledge what you get. If allowing that maybe it's only your imagination makes you feel more comfortable than admitting that you are getting psychic impressions, that's okay. This is only the beginning!

Scientists and Psychics?

Contrary to what may be a popular belief, not all scientists are contraintuitive or, more specifically, skeptical when it comes to psychic abilities. Many, in fact, especially in the medical community, use their psychic senses on a regular basis. Nutritionists, nurses, and even doctors can tune in to their intuition to help them determine what types of foods their patients may need to eat in order to bolster their immune systems or their nutritional values.

For example, if a nutritionist has a patient come in who is looking to increase their daily energy, the nutritionist may tell them to lay off the red meat and increase their iron intake with green leafy vegetables instead. This is not rocket science, as most of us know too much red meat can cause lethargy. In general it is just good nutritional advice. In addition, the specialist may taste the flavor of coffee. Normally, coffee would not be something they might recommend, but in this instance they suggest it for the caffeine, which will help the client with energy as well as their attention deficit disorder. Telling their patient to have more caffeine may go against all of their nutritional recommendations, but by tuning in to their psychic senses they know it will be beneficial, at least in the short term.

Doctors may also tune in to their psychic abilities without recognizing it for what it is. Imagine their patient coming in with the same complaint of experiencing a lack of energy. They feel sluggish and tired more often than not. Where the nutritionist in the previous example may have recommended caffeine based on the phantom coffee taste, the doctor may pick up on something entirely different with his patient.

Knowing that he was already planning to run some tests, including a nutritional workup and a urine analysis, he feels comfortable trusting in the psychic flavor he is getting. He tastes copper. Copper is a very common taste associated with blood. So now, the doctor has an additional direction to go in. He may decide that the psychic hit he's experiencing indicates he needs to get the patient into the hospital right away. There's a definite possibility there's something wrong with his blood; more specifically, his circulatory system, including his heart.

Though the examples I've used are entirely made up, they explain how simply, and possibly how easily, these medical professionals are able to utilize their psychic senses. Though there are many skeptics in the medical or scientific community, there are also many believers—whether they actively pursue it or not.

What Is It Called?

As you make your way happily through this book you'll find some of the chapters will resonate more than others. Chances are your gifts will make themselves known through the exercises and the stories included in every section. And you will love how practicing can help you enhance the senses you are more in tune with as well as the intuitive abilities that haven't been so strong.

This book will help you personally relate to your different psychic senses, and you will be able to identify which gifts come more naturally to you. You will also learn what your intuitive senses are called and what each one helps you with. The words for the psychic senses start with *clair,* which is French for "clear," giving us clear seeing (clairvoyance), clear hearing (clairaudience), clear feeling (clairsentience), clear knowing (claircognizance), clear tasting (clairgustance), clear smelling (clairalience or clairolfaction), clear emotion (clairempathy), and clear touch (clairtangency). You will experience all of these senses in the pages to come. You'll also have an opportunity to explore telepathy and psychokinesis in the final chapters.

Chakras—What Are They?

Chakras—spinning wheels of energy in your etheric body —play a big role in tuning in to your psychic senses, and this book will help explain how they contribute to your intuition. There are seven major energy centers, or spiritual batteries, organized in a rainbow-colored line from the base of your spine, between your legs, all the way up to the top of your head. Each of these chakras corresponds to your psychic senses, and focusing on them may be of great assistance when trying to tune in.

The first three chakras are lower chakras. These are all linked to need, physical desire, and drive. All of your chakras are connected to your psychic abilities. The first chakra, or root chakra, is related to your foundation or your security. It corresponds to your stability, your family, and your sense of community. It is the base chakra, red in color, at the base of your spine. It is also connected to your claircognizance or clear knowing.

The second chakra, or sensual chakra, is orange and is located a couple of inches below the navel. This spiritual energy center is related to your sensuality as well as your sexuality. This chakra plays a role in your feeling or clairsentient abilities.

Your third chakra is your power center and is located in your solar plexus. This yellow energy center is where your gut instincts occur. It is the seat of your clairsentience, and is related to your self-esteem.

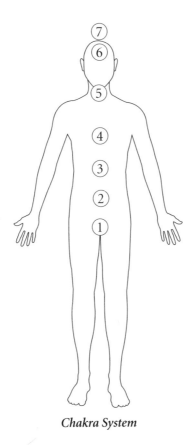

Chakra System

The upper chakras are more closely linked to spirituality and consciousness. Your fourth or green spiritual battery is in your chest and is also known as your heart chakra. This center is related to matters of the heart and love as well as healing of yourself and others.

Your fifth chakra is your communication center. This blue energy area is responsible for channeling messages from the other side and your clairaudience. It's also related to communicating your wants and needs.

The sixth chakra, the indigo center, is your third eye. This is your psychic sight or clairvoyant spiritual energy center.

Finally, your seventh or violet chakra is known as your crown chakra. This important energy center is where your psychic gifts are linked and where your claircognizance sits. It's where all divine guidance is channeled through and where you are connected to the universal energy.

All seven major chakras run smoothly together, feeding off of each other. The chakra system can become off-kilter, which can cause a barrier to opening up your psychic abilities. The system then needs to be realigned. Working with the chakra system while practicing using your psychic senses will help bring them into balance.

Let's Go!

Knowing the terminology will help you label what it is you are tapping into. You don't need to memorize the wording or even understand it right away. While you read this book, you will learn everything you need to know by exercising your psychic abilities. You will learn how to protect yourself from unwanted negativity, open yourself to positive energy, tune in to your intuition, connect to the other side, explore telepathy and psychokinesis, and even discover who you were in a past life! You will have fun, and even surprise yourself, all while enjoying more than sixty exercises. You've inherently got all the tools you need; now you know what to call them and, more importantly, how to utilize them to create a better and more fun life!

This is your time to shine—your chance to sh
you already know to be true. You are a spiritual beinㇰ
in a physical body. You'll find that your intuition does not
negate your logic, but that in fact, your logic helps to ratio-
nalize your intuition! Enjoy every moment of your intuitive
life to the fullest.

Exercise: Protect Yourself!

Before starting any type of intuitive connection it's
important to protect yourself from any negative
energy. The best and easiest way to do this is through
meditation and visualization.

Sit somewhere comfortable with both feet firmly
on the floor. Close your eyes. Feel the bottoms of
your feet where they connect to the floor and the void
where they don't. Focus on the empty space.

Now, imagine the feeling of that empty space as it
travels up and around your body, filling every nook
and cranny, every curve, and the emptiness of matter. Allow this space to be filled with beautiful white
light. As you visualize this light swirling next to you
and around you, feel it getting warmer, brighter, and
more expansive. Push it out farther, about five feet
from your physical body. While you feel the energy
growing, imagine it becoming even lighter and
warmer, leaving no room for any negative energy or
debris to remain or penetrate into your space.

Sit with this energy flowing around you for at
least five minutes. When you feel comfortable, open

your eyes and take a few deep breaths, allowing your energy to stay grounded but continue to surround you.

It's Your Turn

Get ready now. Hold on and enjoy the ride. What you are about to do will surely change your perspective and expose you to a new level, a new dimension of reality. You will learn how to connect to your own intuition, which is more powerful than you can possibly imagine. You will receive guidance, not only from the pages in this book, but from your own personal helpers on the other side, who will enhance your life. Buckle up, it's your turn!

one

What Are Psychic Senses?

"My sixth sense has always been my greatest gift."
—SONIA CHOQUETTE

Psychic senses are the coolest thing since sliced bread. Scratch that. Psychic senses were cool way before sliced bread! When we tap into these mystical abilities, we are given the potential to experience something far greater than we ever could have imagined. Psychic senses open us up to a new dimension of understanding our world and our lives. It is through these intuitions that we gain an in-depth awareness that there is more to this existence than the naked eye can see.

Your Higher Power

Psychic senses are what allow us to receive impressions from the universe that aren't based on anything we can touch.

These impressions are messages from the other side—from spirit guides; angels; our deceased loved ones; and God or Buddha, the universe, or whatever or whoever you believe to be your higher power. This sixth sense is what lets us see, hear, taste, touch, smell, feel, know, and just psychically perceive these communications.

For many who practice religion, this is a tough row to hoe. Have you ever heard the term "Catholic guilt"? In a nutshell, it means you have to believe everything that the Bible, in its Catholic interpretation, tells you to believe. If you don't, or if you don't act accordingly, you should, and usually do, experience a somewhat disproportionate amount of guilt. Almost every religion has its own version of Catholic guilt, especially if it preaches it is the only acceptable religion. You need not feel that guilt when practicing with intuition, as long as you practice for positive reasons. Your intuition is a natural part of your spirit, and even the Bible talks about connecting to God and the angels. You can be religious and also be spiritual. It is your choice, and you should do whatever gives you comfort.

Religion and spirituality are not one and the same. They are inherently different in that religion is based on manmade doctrine or stories transcribed by men, while spirituality is about your own personal connection to the universe and God and every living being on the planet and then some. You do not need to be religious to be spiritual nor do you need to be spiritual to be religious. To this point, His Holiness the Dalai Lama said, "My religion is simple. My religion is kindness." Your beliefs can be, and actually should be, a constantly changing evolution of ideas, thoughts, and feelings. Your higher power is just that—yours.

Exercise: Your Higher Power

Throughout this book I will talk about our connections to the other side. I may use God or the universe as an example, but feel free to insert your own ideas and beliefs. To truly understand where your messages come from, you need to ponder what you believe.

Take a minute to think about what you believe in. Do you believe in God in a traditional sense? Do you believe in Buddha? Do you feel connected to angels? How about spirit guides or even a guardian angel? Do you feel that your loved ones live on in spirit? What about the people who are known as ascended masters, such as Jesus, Buddha, Kwan Yin, and Mother Mary? Do you think our connections are based more on quantum physics and a type of space-time continuum? Does the universe stand out as what brings us together?

Write down your beliefs. What, if anything, resonates with you? Do you feel strongly about one over the other? Do you believe there are multiple messengers? When you imagine yourself asking to connect, who or what do you feel you're asking? Again, there is no wrong answer!

Open to Interpretation

We have to have a way to interpret the impressions we're given. Often, we experience intuitive messages symbolically and need to translate them. Much like deciphering pictograms or even lyrics to a song, interpreting intuitive messages is easier when you've developed your gifts and learned to translate the psychic symbols you receive.

Our messengers from the other side want to help us to understand, so they will send us information in a way that we can interpret. They use whatever means necessary to transmit their messages so we will recognize them.

I recently did a reading for Lori. She sat in my office for an hour, and I relayed to her a good deal of information. But the thing that really gave her the *aha* moment, or the moment when she knew there was no way for me to know the things I was telling her, was when I told her I saw all types of soldiers from different generations. I literally saw, in my mind's eye, soldiers in varying uniforms including Civil War, Revolutionary War, etc.

"Wow! I can't believe this! When I came in for my reading, I asked my angels to have you talk about the soldiers and then I would believe you were really connected," she said with total enthusiasm.

"Well, I feel like they are coming toward you in waves, kind of like you're discovering them," I told her.

"This is incredible. I recently started researching my ancestry, and I've found numerous soldiers from many different wars in my family tree. I can't believe you got them!" she exclaimed.

"That's awesome! Now, I'm also feeling like your great-great-grandfather or someone in his generation is stepping forward, and I'm seeing a steak and iron. So either you are low in iron and you need to eat red meat or your great-great-grandfather, also a soldier, used to work on the railroad driving stakes into the tracks," I laughed.

"I'm not so sure, but I will find out. And I will make sure I add some extra iron to my diet!" she chuckled back.

She left the office with a bunch of answers as well as a few questions. Within the hour I received an e-mail from Lori. "You are never going to believe this. When I got home there was an e-mail from my father. He sent it to me during our session together. He told me that he just unearthed some information about my great-great-grandfather. He was a soldier and he worked for the railroad, building the tracks, hammering the stakes. What are the odds he would send me an e-mail while I was in session with you? Melanie, thank you so much for this. It is truly amazing!"

What is truly amazing to me is that by utilizing my psychic senses I am able to decipher and read the messages sent to me by my guides and the deceased loved ones of my clients. It is also incredible that they are able to share this information in a way I can interpret so I can relay it to my clients and they can understand. I give the other side total credit for this and am fascinated by how well it works when we allow our intuition to open up.

Imagine Tuning In

Most of us come into this world with our external, natural senses: sight, hearing, smell, touch, and taste. But we are also born with internal senses, the clairs that allow us to see beyond physical reality and to know what otherwise couldn't be known. *Clair* is derived from a French word meaning "clear" and is the prefix for all of the psychic senses. By its very name it is suggesting that psychic senses come through clearly, though it is somewhat of a misnomer. More often than not these clair senses are fuzzy or subtle at best. Practicing with them provides us the chance to interpret them more intelligibly.

Living with our physical and metaphysical abilities fully engaged provides us with a fuller, more comprehensive existence. Closing off any of those senses not only does us a disservice, it can also have a detrimental effect on our psyche. Albert Einstein, possessing one of the greatest minds known to humans, said, quite emphatically, "The only real valuable thing is intuition."

When we are young, we are told we can be anything, do anything, accomplish anything. Why then, does our intuition get shut down? Is it because we don't know any better? Or because we stop believing in our gut instincts? Or is it because it's safer to conform and not stand out? Usually, it's a combination of all of the above, with a little bit of skepticism from others, mainly adults, thrown in. As we grow up, we lose the belief that anything magical or unexplainable can be real. We turn to rationalizing and distrusting everything that can't be proven, touched, or seen for ourselves. And then, we grow up some more and realize that intuition is real, but we call it gut instincts or mother's intuition.

Imagine not trusting your gut feelings on a regular basis, or putting aside faith because it can't be proven. This is where your intuition comes in. Without these senses, we'd be spinning blindly with nothing to hold on to. It is our instincts we rely on to get us through crises or that guide us on the correct path to overcoming adversity or challenge. Jawaharlal Nehru, the first prime minister of the Republic of India, said, "A leader or a man of action in a crisis almost always acts subconsciously and then thinks of the reasons for his action." In other words, our subconscious directs us before our conscious has a chance to consider it.

Tuning in to your psychic abilities can help you make sense of your present and your future. It enables you to see distantly in time and space without physically being there. Scott Cunningham explains our longing to connect to our psychic senses: "The motivation for obtaining a glimpse of tomorrow varies with each individual, but the desire itself is as old as human consciousness and our perception of time." (Cunningham, 2003) Your intuition can help you handle stress and point you in the right direction toward achieving happiness. The first step is opening up your awareness by using your natural gifts and enhancing the other gifts. Psychic senses allow you to look beyond the three-dimensional world and into an entirely separate, yet adjunct plane of existence.

Perhaps most importantly, we are being challenged in our current state of affairs to act locally and think globally. As a nation and, more expansively, an entire world, we are facing more than we appear to be able to handle, but we are still required to act with political, social, and economic intelligence. Our own intuition can help provide us with insight into possible directions and answers to our most pressing issues in our personal communities as well as all over the world. Imagine knowing how to heal poverty, global warming, natural resource depletion, economic instability, famine, disease, war, religious persecution, and so much more.

Exercise: What Your Psychic Senses Can Do for You

I named a few areas where your psychic senses can help you. What aspects in your life or the lives of others do you think utilizing your psychic abilities can assist you with? Write them down. Have you experienced any of them personally? Do you know of anyone else who has?

Forrest Gump?

Many years ago I was attending a workshop at the Omega Institute for Holistic Studies. James Van Praagh was teaching an advanced mediumship class to about four hundred students, myself among them. (I don't think I'll ever stop enjoying being a student!) Toward the end of the week, he asked for volunteers to go up on stage and do readings for random audience participants. I didn't volunteer. Others who were sitting around me kept urging me to raise my hand, insisting that I had been "right on" with my readings all week. I never told them I did it professionally because I wanted to just be part of the student group. I simply told them I wanted to give other people a chance to practice.

Silently, I said to myself, "If I'm meant to do this work, I will get picked to go up on stage somehow."

Next thing I knew, there was a woman on stage who didn't mean to volunteer, but she ended up there after asking James a question. She wasn't really sure what she was doing, but James told her to just pick someone and try to connect. She picked me.

Essentially, she said, "I don't know why I picked you, but I felt I had to."

Little did she know I had just talked to my guides and my loved ones on the other side. Sure enough, after she said that, James said, "Well, it's your turn to come up." The universe truly is magical. I challenged it to get me on stage, and it rose to the occasion seamlessly.

So, I took the stage. Although I was a practicing psychic, I wasn't used to performing in front of so many, so I admittedly was a bit nervous. On the walk up, which seemed interminable, I silently asked the universe and my guides, spiritual helpers from the other side, to assist me by sending me information I could detect with my psychic senses. Again, the universe complied.

I began getting messages. I psychically heard, clairaudiently, "Bubba Gump Shrimp," and I felt like I was in the *Forrest Gump* movie. Then, I was clairvoyantly seeing my own cousins who captain their oyster boats. And I was feeling very hot. I wasn't quite sure what any of it meant yet.

I scanned the audience and felt my energy drawn to one particular woman. I asked her, "Do you have a nephew or someone who works for the Bubba Gump Shrimp Company down South?"

As I was asking her, I also clairsentiently felt pain—the kind of pain that comes with what I assumed to be an overdose of drugs.

"Well, I do have a nephew who works on a fishing boat, I believe it's a shrimp boat, in Florida," she replied.

"I think you need to make sure to connect with him. I feel he may be in trouble with drugs," I continued. "Though, I do feel like there's time to help him."

"Wow. I don't know how you knew that, but I was just talking with my sister, his mother, and she said she was a little worried. Thank you so much for that! I will definitely be in touch!"

Many of my psychic senses were tuned in, allowing me to channel the information to the woman who really needed it. James Van Praagh, to his credit, stood back and let me do my thing, apparently nodding his head in approval the whole time. It's great to be validated.

My guides, and those of the woman I was reading for, sent me information I could understand to help me comprehend the messages I needed to share. I perceived them through my psychic senses. Everyone has these senses, and while you will not always use them for the purposes of reading others, once they become part of your life, you will be all the better because of it.

Tuning in will help you be more aware of your surroundings. You'll be increasingly sensitive to the energy around you, and the energy of others and what they're projecting out into the ether. By utilizing these senses, you'll make more informed decisions and become less judgmental of others—less concerned with the mundane details and more appreciative of what truly matters. Your intuition is what helps ground you and keep you in touch with reality. It's time to tune in to it and validate your natural gifts; there's no need to wait. As spiritual author Wayne Dyer said, "Go for it now. The future is promised to no one."

Exercise: Understanding Your Psychic Senses

The best way to get in touch with your psychic abilities is to begin focusing on them.

Get out your journal and turn to a fresh page. Write down whatever impressions you pick up on when you think of each of the following psychic senses. Include how each of the words makes you feel. Do you feel comfortable? Nervous? Happy? Worried? Excited? What thoughts come to mind when you examine each psychic sense? Do the different senses seem to make sense to you? Or not? Which ones are you drawn to? Which ones do nothing for you? What feels right? What, if anything, feels wrong? Also, write down any experiences you can associate with any of the senses. Above all, allow yourself to enjoy how each one feels!

Clairvoyance (clear seeing)
Clairaudience (clear hearing)
Clairsentience (clear feeling or sensing)
Claircognizance (clear knowing)
Clairgustance (clear tasting)
Clairalience/Clairolfaction (clear smelling)

Clairempathy (clear emotion)
Clairtangency (clear touch)
Telepathy
Psychokinesis

Ready or Not, Here They Come!

You've begun tapping into your incredible potential. The possibilities are virtually limitless. You are naturally intuitive and are now opening to all of your psychic senses. These abilities will help guide you on a path traversing all of the ups and downs in what is sure to be a dynamic and informed existence. Are you ready?

two

Clairvoyance (Clear Seeing)

"All the powers in the universe are already ours.
It is we who have put our hands before our eyes
and cry that it is dark."

—SWAMI VIVEKANANDA

W hat? What do you mean you see him? Is he standing there? Oh my God! Is he behind me? Where is
he? What's he doing? What's he wearing?" Teresa asked in a
panic during a psychic reading in my office.

I'd told her I saw her father and that he was coming
through to wish her a happy birthday. This, understandably,
freaked Teresa out. She, like many others, was afraid. She
practically jumped out of her seat.

"Whoa, slow down! It's okay, Teresa. I see him in my
mind's eye, my third eye, my clairvoyant center. I don't
actually see him standing there like a real person." I didn't
explain to her that although I saw Chris, her dad, internally, I
also sometimes see images of people externally or physically

present, though not nearly as often. That would've really put her over the edge.

Clairvoyance, or psychic seeing, is one of the most commonly referred to psychic senses. Many people use the term "clairvoyant" interchangeably with the word "psychic." Though close, you wouldn't be correct. Clairvoyance is only one aspect of intuitive awareness, as there are many other equally grand senses to tap into, but it is definitely a valuable and much-used one. Have you ever heard of the third eye? This is a term used to describe the sixth chakra, the indigo-colored energy center located behind your forehead between your eyes. It is what helps you to see psychically and can be focused on when trying to connect with your clairvoyance, or your mind's eye.

Teresa was right to question whether Chris was actually in the room with us or not. This is a widespread belief, though usually it's wrong. It is more common to intuitively see something or someone within our minds than outside our mind or externally. This occurred with Abby as well, though it was a phone session, so she wasn't afraid.

"I'm seeing a move from Westchester to Long Island, does this make sense?" I asked her. What I actually saw was the map version of Long Island in my mind.

"That's what we are trying to do!" she verified. (Abby wrote to me and let me know they have since made it to Long Island and are very happy.)

"I see so many women around you, almost like a coven, supporting you, helping you with the move, and so much more."

"Oh, that's great! I thought they may be around," Abby said of her many deceased loved ones.

"I'm seeing a very small woman, and what's interesting is there are butterflies all around her! Now, usually I see butterflies for my mom, but I feel like this is a generation above and that the butterflies have particular meaning for you," I told Abby.

This made her cry. She went on to explain her grandmother was only four-foot-eight and had an almost obsessive love for butterflies! Clothes, jewelry, home décor all had butterflies on them—they were everywhere around her at all times.

I saw Abby's little grandmother clearly surrounded by beautiful butterflies. They weren't physically there, near Abby, but they were there in my mind's eye. Most people who experience clairvoyance will have a hard time determining, at first, whether it's their imagination or truly a psychic image. Our imaginary images look very similar to the clairvoyant flashes we sometimes receive in our third eye. Discovering the difference comes with familiarity.

Exercise: Clearing Out the Third Eye

Located centrally within your forehead, above your brows, is the sixth chakra, also identified as the third-eye chakra. It is this space that you use to clairvoyantly receive any psychic impressions. As with anything that doesn't get used on a regular basis, it has to be cleared periodically to get rid of the cobwebs!

Lie back and get comfortable, being sure you won't be disturbed. Invoke your protective bubble of energy, allowing it to surround you and fill you, keeping you free from any negativity or negative energy.

Close your eyes. Now, focus on your forehead. Be aware of the space between your eyes, above the bridge of your nose. Pay attention to what it feels like. Notice if it is bright or dark, warm or cool. Observe any images that may come to mind when you're concentrating on your third eye.

Next, imagine that right above your third eye are windshield wipers and allow them to begin moving, slowly cleaning your clairvoyant chakra center. As they do, press your finger and thumb together and imagine you are releasing windshield wiper fluid to help your wipers work even better. Allow the wipers to stop when you are sure your third eye is perfectly clear.

Again, pay attention to what that area feels like. Is it any brighter? Or even darker? Has it changed at all? Has the temperature changed? What images do you see now?

Give yourself a few moments to take everything in. When you are ready, open your eyes and immediately write down everything you can remember from both before and after using your wipers. Make note of any differences as well as any similarities. Do you feel any different? Was it comfortable? Uncomfortable? Exciting? Boring? Write it all down.

You can refer back to this exercise anytim
want for help in tuning in to your clairvoyance
clear out any blocks in your third-eye chakra.

Validate Me!

One of the easiest ways to determine whether what you're seeing is merely your own thought or is instead truly a psychic vision, is to put it out there so you can be given feedback. In the beginning, when you are first discovering your awareness, it's encouraging to have validation that what you are receiving as an intuitive image is real and not just a figment of your imagination.

There is, among many, sometimes the belief that you don't need to know whether you are right or not, you just need to give what you get. I'm throwing my hat in to say this is not a great idea for people just starting out. In order to develop further, you need to know you're somewhat accurate; otherwise it's all guesswork. Once you've gotten to the place where you are as comfortable with your sixth sense as you are when you're wearing flannel pajamas, then, and only then, should you throw caution to the wind and believe in the truthfulness of your visions. Validation enhances confidence, which in turn will continue to increase the recognition of your psychic flashes. And more importantly, it'll feel awesome! This does not mean, however, that you should give up if you're not validated 100 percent of the time. One psychic hit is enough to prove you are on to something!

Toward the beginning of my professional psychic career, I was on stage doing mediumship (talking to the dead) in front of about three hundred people. What I saw was very clear, yet confusing at the same time. I received clairvoyant flashes of a yellow truck driving and then flipping upside down. I also saw, in my third eye, a young man with big, black, clunky boots and a jean jacket. And I got the letter *A*. Now, usually when I do a gallery-type event, like this one, I will narrow down the location of the person I'm reading for by using my clairsentience (psychic feeling) and determining which area of the audience he or she is sitting in. This time was no different, except I was able to go right to the person I felt I was attaching to. The only problem was, Dawn, the audience member, denied it.

"That's not for me," she said with defiance.

"Are you sure? I'm being drawn to you and I even see you holding his hand before the accident. I'm also getting the name Aaron or something close to that?" I continued, confident that would trigger Dawn's memory.

"Nope, I don't know what you're talking about. I have no idea," she stated, causing me some confusion.

"Really? Because it really feels like he's coming to tell you he's okay and that he wishes you well in your marriage. Unless this is for someone else?" I asked, scanning the room for any other takers.

By now the audience members were buzzing. Was I off? Did I not interpret this correctly? My confidence was taking a huge hit and I was concerned I was wrong and that it would affect me moving forward with other readings. I normally believed in my visions, if not 100 percent, then at least 80 percent. This was making my belief dip down to about 25 percent.

"Okay, well, I'm not sure, but I do sense there will be an explanation soon to come because I feel like this poor young man tragically passed and is missed by many, including a brother. I'm seeing Aaron wave goodbye to you and his brother. Maybe this will make sense in the future," I finished up, unsure of myself.

The workshop continued and the rest of it went smoothly, nothing to be concerned about, but the visions I'd had representing Aaron and the truck still bothered me. That is, until the girl I was pointing out came up to me afterward.

"I'm sorry. That was for me. I just wasn't ready to publicly acknowledge it," Dawn said. "That's why I came here, to say goodbye and get his approval to move on and marry my fiancé. Aaron and I had a special bond, and he died before we could get married. I loved him so much and miss him, but I need to move on."

"Wow! Thank you so much for validating that for me! I was beginning to think it was just my imagination! So, does the description of him and the truck match?" I asked.

"Everything matched. He flipped his truck and died, and he always wore black Dr. Marten's—big, clunky boots—and a jean jacket. He has a younger brother who was hoping to hear from him as well. It was all perfect," Dawn continued with a tear in her eye.

"Thank you, thank you, and thank you for being brave enough to come to me. I know Aaron appreciates your recognition as well. And congratulations on your upcoming marriage! He says he will be there with bells on!"

The validation I received from Dawn helped me by letting me know it wasn't my imagination. It encouraged me to continue doing my work and to believe in what I was seeing. Sure enough, a few months later I received a message from Dawn that during her wedding ceremony they heard bells tinkling but didn't know where the sound was coming from. Of course, she and I knew it was Aaron.

What Do You See?

You may see images with your third eye that appear like photographs or they may show up like movies. I even have images appear on occasion much like silent, old-time, black-and-white films. There usually is no clearly defined visual you can count on to let you know what you're receiving is real. Realizing you're being shown an intuitive picture comes with being open, believing, and, dare I say it, practice.

The psychic images I received during the reading when Aaron came through were not necessarily precise images of what Aaron looked like or even what the car looked like when he was alive. Instead, I believe what I saw clairvoyantly were symbolic representations of what Aaron needed me to see in order to get the messages through. I received flashes of a tall young man, and separately I saw the shoes and jacket. Then I saw a short, movielike clip of a friend I went to high school with who died when he flipped his car over twenty years ago.

Now, there were definitely differences between the psychic visions and the reality of Aaron's life. But I got the pictures so I could accurately share the message with his old love. For instance, the car my old friend drove was a red sports car. The truck Aaron had flipped was yellow. I knew, using my claircognizance, or clear knowing (see chapter 5), that it was a yellow truck versus a red sports car, though the initial communications that came through my third eye showed me the red car. The truth is, more often than not, the intuitive visions will not always match the physical reality but will instead be representative or symbolic of what our guides, deceased loved ones, and other helpers will use to get their messages across.

Exercise: When Is a Car Really a Truck?

It's time to open up your third eye! I think it's safe to say most of you have a car or have at least ridden in a car or a truck before. For this exercise, you need to be in a comfortable position, somewhere you won't be disturbed, and have your journal and a pen ready. The first thing you need to do is invoke your light by using the protection exercise from the introduction. This will help keep any negativity from creeping its way in and make your experience a positive one.

After you've done that, it's time to begin visualizing. Close your eyes and put your hand up to your forehead. With your fingers, touch the spot right in the center, above your eyebrows. Some people have an area that seems a bit softer and even recessed. Place your fingers and your attention gently there. Take a deep breath and feel the warmth that is beginning to spread, generating from your third eye, your clairvoyant center.

With your fingers remaining on your forehead, think about what your car or your family car or a friend's car looks like. Notice first the color of the outside and the shape. Is it more than one color? Can you see the wheels? What color are the rims? Can you see the back window? Is there a windshield wiper? Are there any bumper stickers or window decals? Do you notice any dings, dents, or scratches? Make a mental note of everything you see as you slowly walk around the car in your mind.

Now, it's time to go inside. What color is the interior? Are there different colors? How many seats are there? What type of material are the seats? Where is the gear shifter? Is it standard or automatic? What does the dashboard look like? What gauges are there? Is there a sunroof? Do you see a navigation system or a DVD player? Is there a different type of screen? What about a stereo or speakers? What color is the rug? Are there floor mats? Are there any pockets in the doors or the seats? Any baby seats? What else do you notice about the interior? Again, make a mental note of everything you see and all that you remember. And then take a few deep breaths.

Now, think of a different car, possibly one of your friend's cars that you know they have but you've never been inside of, or think of a car that you've always wanted or that you like the look of. Make sure this "dream" car is one you can go see, either at someone's house or at a dealership.

Go through the same process, this time using your psychic vision instead of your memory. With your fingers no longer covering your third eye, tune in to the color or colors of the outside and the shape. What color are the rims? Do you see lettering on the tires? Is the back window plain or are there antenna lines or defroster lines? How about a windshield wiper? Are there any letters or bumper stickers or window decals? Is the paint free from dings, dents, or scratches? Make a mental note of everything you see clairvoyantly as you slowly walk around the car in your mind's eye.

Next, go inside. Is the interior all one color or different colors? How many seats are there and what type of material are they made of? Any baby seats? Is it standard or automatic? Do you see a clutch? What does the dashboard look like? What gauges are there on the instrument panel? Is there a sunroof or a moonroof? Do you see a navigation system, DVD player, or backup camera? Can you see the stereo or speakers? What color is the rug? Are there any floor mats? Are there any pockets in the doors or the seats? What else do you notice about the interior? Again, make a mental note of everything you see. And then slow down and take a few deep breaths.

Without thinking about it, open your eyes and begin recording everything you can about what you psychically saw in the dream car. The more details, the better. Include everything, even if you were unsure of what you saw. If you want, you can also write down what you remembered from your own car on a differ-ent page in your journal. This may help to trigger any of the psychic sights you saw in the dream car but are forgetting about.

After you've done that, go on a field trip to find that car! If it's a friend's, check out the inside as well as the outside. If it is at a dealer, you may have to look at a few different versions of the car to have it make sense to you. How well did you do? How many details seem to fit? Were you right on? Way off? If you didn't get anything right, it may mean you need a lot more practice working with your third eye. If you got about 50 percent correct, you are averaging out, and the more you practice, the more fun it will be. If you got higher than that, this may be your prevalent psychic sense! Practice more using different cars or even trucks—you may find you become really good at tapping into your third eye!

Interpreting Basic Symbols

What came first? The egg? Or, well, the egg? In one of my previous books, *The Book of Psychic Symbols: Interpreting Intuitive Messages*, I wrote about a reading I did in which I saw eggs, regular chicken eggs, dropping to the floor rhythmically, one at a time. The eggs, I realized, represented my client's time was running out to have children, which she had just been discussing with her fiancé that morning. I recently did another reading for someone else. And yes, there were more eggs. But this time it was the first thing I saw, and they were lined up as far as I could see, in plain white cartons.

"So, I'm seeing cartons of eggs. The last time I saw eggs was because someone wanted a baby. Either you are pregnant or this represents fertility or it's about lots of babies in possibly some other way," I explained to my client Karyn during a phone session. "Do you understand this?"

"No. I'm not pregnant, and I'm not expecting to be considering my husband had a vasectomy!" she laughed.

"Hmmm … allergic? Although, I really think it has to do with being fertile or something. Does this make sense?" I continued. I knew it had to mean something if it was one of the first things I was seeing. I saw, in my third eye, carton after carton of white eggs, lined up, fading off into the distance.

"I really don't know what it could be," Karyn answered.

"Okay, well. Hold on to it. Maybe it will mean something to you later," I told her, knowing that in some way it was significant.

We continued the reading, and within a couple of minutes we figured it out. After telling her other things that came to me, I discovered what it was. Turns out it was a huge part of her life. She was an ob-gyn who helped women with fertility and delivered babies!

"Oh my goodness! I wasn't even thinking of that. I can't believe I didn't realize the significance of what you were seeing when you first brought it up. It's funny how our occupations just become what we do, and the significance of them starts to fade into the background," Karyn exclaimed. "Wow!"

Wow was right. I didn't actually see her in her white lab coat in her office with her clients. Instead, I saw eggs, which symbolically indicated to me it was connected with fertility or babies. If I had let it go, or discounted it, we never would've gotten to the bottom of what my psychic vision was referring to. Believing in what I knew to be a true impression was crucial in bringing out the information to Karyn, which let her know I was tuned in to her energy.

What I saw psychically, the egg cartons lined up into the distance, was obviously symbolic and not literal. It did not indicate she had an infinite number of eggs at home in her refrigerator or that she worked in an assembly line packaging eggs. It also didn't mean she was a chicken! It was, however, an important part of my reading for her because it helped me understand who she was and what she did and that it was a significant aspect of her life. Seeing symbols can be tricky sometimes—it's difficult to tell whether what you are clairvoyantly seeing is real or just representative of something else. It's essential to practice interpreting some basic psychic symbols so you can be prepared and know what they mean if you see them. In almost every reading I do for my clients, I am given these pictures in my mind's eye, each one holding a multitude of information. Even more incredible is that at least one in three readings shows me a new symbol that seems to pop up in subsequent readings. That's why it is without a doubt an important part of learning to tune in to your psychic sight.

Exercise: Symbolically Speaking

With your journal in hand, get comfortable. Allow yourself enough time and multiple pages for this next exercise. Then, close your eyes and breathe deeply. Inhale positive energy and exhale any negativity you may have trapped inside your body, min or spirit. Do this for at least three minutes, releasin any stress or tension.

Now, imagine a bubble of white light traveling through you and around you, protecting you, keeping all distractions and negative energy away from you. Push the bubble outward, mentally creating a barrier of love between you and the outside world.

Move your attention to the top of your head. Imagine the shape of a cone forming, its tip beginning at the top of your crown, or your crown chakra, and funneling upward toward the sky. This funnel is a beautiful, silvery violet color and is buzzing with energy. It is also brimming with information that is significant to you and the symbols you are about to discover.

Open your eyes now, still relaxed, the cone still there, and pick up your pen. One by one, record the following common symbols and then, using your funnel as the channeling path, write down whatever information you psychically see for each symbol. Feel free to draw the symbol as well. This may give you an even clearer picture.

Airplane
Angel
Bear
Bicycle
Bird
Boat
Book

Butterfly

Car

Cat

Chair

Church

Computer

Cup

Desk

Dog

Dragonfly

Eagle

Egg

Fire

Flower

Food

Foot

Fountain

Grass

Hawk

House

Ice

Knife

Light

Lion

Moon

Pen

Person

Phone

Picture

Radio
Rock
Roller coaster
Sky
Stairs
Star
Stove
Sun
Telephone
Waterfall

After you are all done recording your symbolic translations, go back and reread them. Do they make sense to you? Are they all straightforward? Or, do some have meanings you normally wouldn't have associated with them? Study them and notice if any other images come to you as you psychically interpret these symbols with your third eye.

Keep these symbolic references in your journal as well as your mind; you never know when they will come in handy. Now that you understand how to translate these visual images, any future symbols will be that much easier to interpret.

Literal or Symbolic, Sometimes Stuff Really Is Just Stuff

Now that you are aware of what it means to receive a psychic or clairvoyant image as a symbol, it's essential to know when it's a symbol or something literal. This can be a tough call.

For example, if you are wondering if you should grab something to bring home for lunch for your children from the store and you see a jar of jelly in your mind's eye, does that mean you should bring it home? Or are you seeing the jelly to represent the kids already ate? Sometimes it's more about trusting your gut instinct than trying to decipher the symbol. I have to say, though, from many ignored occurrences, if you are walking through the grocery store and intuitively get a flash of jelly, buy it! I can't tell you how many times I've gone home to a husband standing there with the peanut butter, bread, and knife, but no jelly.

All of the clairvoyant images you'll see come with some type of background. Again, you may experience the vision as if looking at a movie, a photo, or a filmstrip. You may see full color or even black and white. All of the psychic pictures will be in a setting. This is what helps me determine whether I am seeing a symbolic message or a literal image.

Clairvoyance does not follow definitive rules. Your third eye can and will surprise you and keep you on your toes. There are no absolutes. But often when I receive a psychic image, I'm able to distinguish whether it's symbolic because of how it feels clairsentiently (see chapter 4) or because there is detail in the image I'm clairvoyantly seeing. If there is only a solid color background behind the vision, it can often indicate it is representative. For example, when I see a bicycle almost floating with no other color or detail, it is usually symbolic. But if I psychically see a bicycle, with the ground under it and a yard behind it and possibly other bikes around it, it may indicate to me it is more of a literal message. Pay attention to the background.

Another way to determine when you're having a clairvoyant occurrence is to understand whether you are experiencing a subjective or objective episode. Often, though not always, if what you are seeing is subjective, or existing in your mind or thinking mind, it is more your imagination or memory. If it is an objective vision, or appearing as if it's outside of your physical thought, an object you are looking at on the outside (even though in your mind's eye) it is a psychic impression. This can be very difficult to discern, even for the professional psychic, and clarity is usually only achieved through practice.

I did a reading for Grayson. She came in to my office without any specific goal in mind besides learning what I picked up about her psychically. After going over a lot of basic information, I tuned in to something different. It was very simple but very telling for her. It was her *aha* moment. I saw, clairvoyantly, that her mother helped occasionally with Grayson's children. And I took it a step further by telling her that her mother was frustrated by all of the piles of stuff in the house. What I saw were piles of mail, magazines, clothes, toys, and even discarded items. These piles were significant to Grayson because they were all over her house. I knew the piles were part of her home because I saw surrounding details, like walls and furniture. I also saw them objectively, meaning I saw them as if I was looking at them rather than being part of them or part of the object. Even though Grayson was happy about me providing her with the evidence that I was really psychically seeing her house, she was not happy that I could see her piles! I had to tell her not to worry; I am a much better psychic than housecleaner myself!

As shown with Grayson's reading, seeing the piles subjectively, or outside of my imagination, even though they were seen with my third eye, helped me know it was literal as opposed to symbolic. Sometimes it's easy to discern; other times it's not. The most important thing to remember about clairvoyance is to be open to the images; don't discount what you see.

Exercise: Is This for Real?

It's your turn to not only practice your clairvoyance but also try and differentiate between symbolic visions and literal images. Get ready—it's going to be fast!

As usual, protect yourself first. Then, sit in front of the television (turned off) with your journal and a pen. Before you turn the television on, tune in to the energy of the TV. Now, write down what you think will be on the screen when you turn it on. As you are tuning in, make sure you are tapping into what will be there when you actually switch on the television and not what's on it as you are writing down the information. You need real time.

It's important now to note specifics to determine whether you are seeing the literal picture or the symbolic picture. For example, if you clairvoyantly see a man, write that down. But if you are seeing Brad Pitt, write that down. You may find that the man is symbolic of whatever man is on the screen when you turn it on, or that Brad Pitt is symbolic of an attractive or even a sexy man. You may also find that

Brad Pitt is literally the man on the television channel when you turn it on. That will be the key to understanding whether you're symbolically and literally seeing with your psychic vision. There is no wrong way; clairvoyance comes in many forms.

Try it again. Maybe you see a car this time. Describe it. When you switch the TV on, is it the same car? Or a different type and/or color car? Again, this helps you understand symbolism versus realism. Keep trying by changing the channel. Remember, for most of your psychic exercises, don't think or doubt what you are seeing, just go with it!

Don't be discouraged if you didn't hit on what was on the channel. Keep practicing. It may take time to develop your clairvoyant abilities. If you did see the images correctly, congratulations! You are well on your way!

Toning Your Clairvoyant Muscles

We are all intuitive. Yes, I'm sure you've heard that before. But it's true. We really are. However, we are not all ready to be professional psychics, nor do we want to be, for that matter. Developing your clairvoyance is like developing any other muscle you have in your physical body. You need to work with it regularly to have it work with you. Most people have to guide their rational mind to not only see but also understand the visions they are receiving. Your budding talents rarely just appear with perfect clarity; usually they are more subtle and require training to fully comprehend.

Clairvoyance, being one of the most popular or well-known psychic abilities, is like that for a reason. Sometimes it's easier to recognize the visions because we've already become accustomed to seeing visions in our mind. We all have an imagination. All of us can conjure up images on demand. Clear seeing is like an extension of that; it's the ability to see images that are coming from external sources such as our guides and deceased loved ones.

Clairvoyance is also one of the senses that tend to overlap with other psychic senses. For example, if you are experiencing clairaudience, or clear hearing (see chapter 3), you may see images to clarify or reinforce what you are psychically getting. Clairgustance (see chapter 6) will allow you to smell something that's not physically there and your third eye will lock that smell down with images to help you understand what it is. Psychic vision is definitely a primary psychic sense, but it's kind of an adjunct one as well. It's an all-around sense that needs to be exercised in order to stay fresh and available at all times.

Whether you are primarily clairvoyant or not, your third eye needs to be opened to interpret the messages you're being psychically shown. These messages can be as simple as a single flash of color or as complicated as watching rolling movie imagery. Just think of how many visual cues you receive on a regular basis with just your physical sight; then imagine how many you can get with your psychic sight. It's unlimited. Practicing seeing with your third eye will absolutely help you to open it up now and for the future. It will take time and effort, but just think of the benefits. You will be rewarded with a glimpse into a world that you may have previously been unaware of; you are now privy to the ancient powers of clairvoyance!

Exercise: Picture This

At the risk of sounding redundant, protect yourself! Do your protection exercise to keep you free from any negative energy that may be nearby. Then, find a friend.

Have your friend take five envelopes and put a picture, a drawing, or something with detail into each of them. Have each of them be different. For example, a picture of Grandma inside her house is fine, but tell your friend not to put another picture of Grandma inside her house in another envelope. Instead have them put a cat prowling the yard or even a Chinese food menu or a birthday card in the next envelope. Make sure the colors, imagery, and even the feel of the pictures are not all the same. Having said that, you can't know what is going into each of the envelopes.

Now, have your friend shuffle all of the envelopes so they don't know which is which. We don't want them sending you clairaudient or clairsentient vibes. Then, have him or her hold up, one at a time, each envelope for you to tune in to. Imagine you can see what's inside. Write down every detail you see with your third eye. What are the colors? Are there people? What are they wearing? Is there more than one person? What objects are in the picture? What shapes are there? Do you see anyone you know? Are you familiar with the photograph or the objects or the people in it? Is it something other than a photograph? Can you "see" the temperature by the images? For example, snow, fall leaves, pool, etc. Write down all of the details.

After you are done with the first one, have your friend take the picture out of the envelope. Does it match what you saw? If yes, great! If not, why? Look at each detail you recorded. Do the colors look close to what you saw? Are any of the shapes the same? Give yourself credit for any similarities you see. If you wrote down a cheetah with yellows and oranges all over and brown spots and it turned out to be a field with yellow, orange, and brown sunflowers, great! You are getting the imagery; now it's time for the details.

If you didn't get anything at all, try the next envelope. After you are done, compare what you've written with what was in the envelope. If you did get something, keep going and don't stop until you are done with all of the pictures. You may find it gets easier with each envelope to describe in full what you see with your third eye.

Again, don't get discouraged regardless of how correct your interpretation was! Have your friend shuffle the pictures again and pick one. This time, though, have them look at the picture and focus on sending you the image with their imagination. Let them stare at the image and psychically transmit it to you. Do this for all five before you compare.

Does having your friend send you the picture make it easier or harder? Or was there no difference? Did the images come in more or less clearly? Did you find yourself jumping to conclusions because you know your friend? Despite the outcome, continue practicing this whenever you can to flex those third-eye muscles!

Sometimes Seeing Is Believing

For some people, seeing is believing. They need to see with their physical eyes in order to believe that something is possible. Believing in a reality or the possibility of something is usually easier with visual evidence, but interpreting correctly just what it is that is being seen is not always simple. Understanding what it is you're viewing generally comes with knowledge of what the people, places, or things you are seeing are.

Often, it goes beyond understanding and straight to having confidence that perhaps something can be real even if you don't actually see it. Believing in the clairvoyant visions inside your mind without ever truly having any external vision to match up with them is a hard pill to swallow if you're not sure that what you're seeing is genuine. Even for professional psychics there is usually some level of doubt or questionability. Most skilled intuitives hold a healthy degree of skepticism.

Around the time my first daughter was born, I questioned my psychic ability. I mean, really. If I was truly psychic, why wasn't I able to see the lottery numbers?! And why couldn't anyone else? I mean, I realized everyone was not meant to win or be rich, but I could be. I was convinced. My logical mind kicked in after that, and I came to the conclusion that for some reason I was not meant to intuit the lottery numbers; that obviously was not part of my life lesson this time around (though I haven't given up hope that it is still possible!). Having gotten through that somewhat critical questioning stage brought me face-to-face with another. If I was able to communicate psychically and see things in my third eye internally, why wasn't I seeing anything externally?

When my mother was alive, toward the end of her human existence, we talked about her own personal experiences. Soon after her sister died of breast cancer, my mother was going through her sister's clothes to figure out what to do with everything. Some things she knew she would keep, but others Mom wasn't so sure about. That is, until Aunt Jeanne showed up at the foot of her bed and began directing her.

"That would look really nice on Mom," Aunt Jeanne told my mother, speaking about my grandmother. "And you should just donate that. I never liked it anyway!" she continued.

Item by item she instructed my mother, giving her reasons as to why each item should be placed with whomever or should be donated. When I asked my mom if she listened to Aunt Jeanne, she replied with a somewhat disturbed chuckle, "Of course, absolutely—to every last detail. There was no way I wasn't going to listen to her!"

Linda, my mom, had another somewhat chilling yet comforting experience. Right around the same time my

Aunt Jeanne had passed, Mom's fiancé, Al, died as well. It was definitely a rough time for her. She shared with me a very special moment.

"I was lying in bed and crying, much like I had been doing for months. I asked for some direction or some closure so I could move on," she told me.

This was difficult for her, as her faith in God was somewhat disrupted by the lack of support she had experienced after her separation from my father. That, along with her scientific background in medicine, was enough to leave a bad taste in her mouth. After all, she couldn't understand how she saw so many countless lives lost during her forty-something years as a critical care nurse.

Almost immediately she heard someone say her name, almost in a whisper. "Linda."

"I opened my eyes and there was Al. He was standing at the foot of the bed, just like your Aunt Jeanne had," Mom explained.

"Wow. Were you scared?" I had asked her.

"No, it was actually very comforting. He just told me he loved me and that he was very sorry, but he had to go. I could feel him there. Seeing him was the icing on the cake."

The stories my mother shared with me inspired me to question my own experience. If I was to do this work and believe it was true, I needed more. At the time, I was studying angelic communication, but I questioned their existence. How would I know it was truly real if I only saw them in my mind's eye? I decided that I needed to see an angel, physically, externally, outside of my body. Then, and only then, would I really be sure. It wasn't that I fully doubted the presence of energy or the ability to communicate, I just knew I had to witness the form of an actual angel to fully acknowledge them as beings.

That night I awoke from a deep sleep. Not because I heard my baby calling out or crying, and not even because I had to use the bathroom, which of course was very common. No, this was something different. I felt as though I was willed to open my eyes. In the darkness, in the distant corner of the room at the very top of the stairs, stood an angel. I didn't see it in full color or like I would a human being. I saw its shape and its shadow in full form, huge wings and all. It stood, though I don't remember it having feet, about six and a half feet tall, large by anyone's standards. It it didn't move; it just watched me from its place above the stairwell.

I felt no fear, no worry. I was not confused at all. Instead, what I was looking at created a degree of comfort and gave me that additional confirmation that what I was doing, this whole psychic thing, was for real. It was kind of like an "ask and you shall receive" gift that I didn't really expect. Seeing the lottery numbers didn't feel quite as essential anymore. I had been given one of the greatest gifts the universe had—I had seen an angel—and for me, seeing truly was believing.

Just because I was able to see an angel, a very stereotypical one at that, doesn't mean you will automatically be able to if you ask for it. We all receive incredible visions at different times in our lives, sometimes without recognizing them for what they are. The key is to learn to understand them.

Exercise: Do You See What I See?

Now, it's your turn. What would it take for you to believe? Think of something you'd really like to see, externally, but with your clairvoyance. It could be an angel, like I did, or it could be an answer to a question you may have.

For example, you may be looking for direction as to whether or not to do something. If, as has happened to me before, you're driving down the road and see a billboard that says, "If you're waiting for a sign, this is it!" I'd say that counts! If you're hoping to see a loved one, allow symbolic representations to count. For instance, extraordinary daisies in an unusual location may be your vision on behalf of your mom, Daisy. Or, if your best friend that you played lacrosse with has died and you want to know he is still around, don't discount the bouncing ball you thought you imagined going down the stairs that disappeared. Chances are that was your external vision.

Now, the only thing you need to do is come up with your question, or your ask, and then be patient. You may have something happen right away or it may take weeks to have your clairvoyance validated. Seeing is believing, but remember, it's not the most typical form of clairvoyance. If it doesn't happen for you, don't be discouraged. Allow yourself to continue to be open to the possibility!

Using Your Extra Set of Eyes

Your clairvoyance affords you the opportunity to use not only your physical eyes but also your third eye. You may find that the combination of the two gives you a greater perspective into everything in your life and enhances your overall perception. Clean those lenses. From here on out you will be seeing more clearly!

three

Clairaudience (Clear Hearing)

*"Inner guidance is heard like soft music in the night
by those who have learned to listen."*

—VERNON HOWARD

Clairaudience, or clear hearing, is the ability to hear things psychically without the use of your physical ears. Does hearing something that's not physically there make you crazy? Or does it simply mean that you are tuning in to the other side? We all hear something that isn't there at some point in our lives. Learning how to decipher those sounds or those messages is what keeps us from feeling like we are going insane. It separates us from those who don't tap into their intuition. Sometimes those interpretations can be a little off, even for someone like me who reads for people professionally.

"Is there somebody in your family who was a cowboy?" I asked my client Jen.

"No. Not that I can think of," she responded.

"Really? Because I can't help but think that I'm picking up something to do with cowboys," I continued.

I kept hearing a song repeat over and over in my head, but I couldn't quite get a grasp on what song it was. The melody was evading me. I knew, however, it had something to do with cowboys or the Wild West.

"Are you sure you didn't have someone pass who was a cowboy? It feels like a father figure to me," I carried on.

"Honestly, I can't imagine what you're talking about. There were no cowboys in my family," Jen insisted.

"I keep hearing the theme song from that old TV show *Rawhide*, and I'm hearing the name John Wayne," I told her. "So it either has to do with cowboys or it has to do with one of my uncles who were named John and Wayne."

"Oh my goodness. I know exactly what you're talking about! My father was always watching old Westerns. It was something that he was known for. It makes perfect sense that you'd be hearing that song. He loved those kinds of movies!" she exclaimed excitedly.

"I knew there had to be a reason that it kept playing in my head. This is his way of coming through to let you know it's really him," I told her, relieved that we were able to figure it out.

She understood the message in the nick of time. I was just about to ask her about role-playing in the privacy of her bedroom! I couldn't for the life of me figure out what else it could've been. Yeehaw!

Hearing songs or lyrics is very common with clairaudience. Often there are people who are associated with specific songs; people in your family or people you are friends with. This is their way of letting you know that it's really them coming through.

Hearing a song does not necessarily mean that you hear everything about the song or that you hear the full song. You may just hear the lyrics to the song, or you may just hear the melody to the song. Often, this may be an indication that someone from the other side is around you. Take, for example, my mom in her younger years. She loved the band Boston. Anytime I hear "More Than a Feeling" or another song by that band, I identify that it's her way of letting me know everything's good and that she's around. That's not the only music she's known for though.

While driving home from getting our family Christmas tree a few years ago, we were flipping through CDs and my husband popped one in the stereo. Andrea Bocelli started belting out his version of "O Holy Night" and I began crying.

"Mommy, it's okay," Samantha, my younger daughter, said.

"She always cries for this song, especially because it's Andrea Bocelli," Molly, my older daughter, responded, as there was no way I could speak.

When she was a teenager, my mom and her high school choir recorded their Christmas concert and "O Holy Night" became the official start of Christmas during my childhood. Then, as my mom got older, she let go of everything wrong or negative in her life while listening to Andrea Bocelli. Now, if I hear his incredible voice or that magical song with my psychic hearing, I tear up because I know that it's more of a specific message from her that she loves me.

More often than not the music that reminds you of somebody will come through just to let you know that they are okay and they hear or see what you're going through. You may hear the music in your head to help you make a choice or a decision. It doesn't really matter whether you hear the lyrics or the actual tune, as long as you're able to recognize what the song is and what it means.

My husband, Tom, is very big on asking me if his business is going well. He is a custom cabinet maker and works with many high-end clients building beautiful kitchens, libraries, living rooms, and more. He has never advertised and gets all of his jobs by word-of-mouth. This also means there are times when his business is slow; never so slow that he would close up shop, but slow enough that he becomes a little concerned. That's when he asks the dreaded question, "What do you get about the business? Is more work coming in?"

"I keep hearing the song 'Everything's Gonna Be All right,'" I usually respond. This has become the norm for us. As long as I hear that song, I know that everything will work out. He's also begun hearing that song. Whether it's for new jobs coming in or it's more general regarding our financial situation, if either of us hears the lyrics to that song we know that everything will work out in time and we need to just keep going.

The music itself isn't important. What is important is knowing and understanding that a particular type of music or song represents an answer, a person, or a loved one from the other side. It may be a song from the radio or a song that you used to dance to that you remember from when they were alive. This is obvious and makes perfect sense.

The music you hear may even have something to do with their heritage. Take for example the bagpipes. Quite often if I'm trying to psychically receive a location or talk about a vacation destination or even connect to somebody who's passed, I may hear the bagpipes to indicate Ireland or even Scotland. It doesn't necessarily mean that the person had to play the bagpipes or that they ever even listened to bagpipe music. Instead, it's just a reference for me. Whether it's a song from the radio or a musical instrument, deciphering it becomes easier with practice.

Daphne was in my office recently for a reading. Normally when I do readings, I channel information before my client even arrives and I write it all down. Describing and talking about these messages I've received usually takes up the full hour's session and can run the gamut from hair color of the sitter to specific communications from their dead relatives. Often, the messages I get mean absolutely nothing to me, but I record it because I know what may be meaningless to me probably means something important to them. Such was the case with Daphne.

I was given all types of information, but one thing that stood out was the song "Hot N Cold" by Katy Perry. I kept hearing it over and over again with my clairaudience. I realized, as I began telling Daphne about it, that it wasn't any of the other lyrics that were significant; rather, it was the title— it was all about what was going on with her. It described her personality as well as her relationship. That helped us get right to the root of the reading.

Physically hearing the music when you've asked for some kind of a sign or symbol to let you know that your deceased love ones are around you is also a form of recognition. Once you've discovered what the music or song is, you may find yourself beginning to notice that particular music playing when you are thinking about them or that the music plays and it reminds you of them. This just helps to reinforce your connection to them and the possibility that they are trying to connect to you.

Exercise: Sing It, Baby

Be sure you are somewhere that's very comfortable and where you will not be disturbed. Also, try to be somewhere that's quiet—you don't want to be distracted by other sounds, noises, or vibrations for this exercise. Close your eyes and take a nice deep breath.

As with the previous chapters, imagine a beautiful, bright bubble surrounding you and protecting you from any negativity. Allow that bubble to expand farther and farther, and as it does imagine that there is a warm energy buzzing through you and around you, stimulating your senses and opening you up to receive messages. As that warm energy fills you, allow it to push that bubble out; stretching and protecting you even more.

Think about one of your closest friends. Imagine being with them and listening to the radio. Watch them as they use their hands to change the station and tune in to the perfect melody for them. It's okay if they have to press a couple buttons or change their iPod or cell phone to play just the right song. Allow yourself now to use that clear hearing to listen to the music that is playing. Do you hear the lyrics? Do you hear just the melody? Or can you hear the whole song? Do you get only a snippet of information or is the entire musical selection being played out in full?

Go ahead and open your eyes now and get out your journal. Write down the name of your friend and the song that you heard. Does it make sense to you? Is it a song that's familiar to you? Is it a song that would normally make you think of your friend? Or is it a song that is entirely different from one that you would've expected? There is no right or wrong answer. If you heard more than one song, make sure you record everything. Write down whether you heard the lyrics or the music or the entire song. Did it sound like it was coming from inside your head? Or did it sound like it was coming from somewhere outside your body?

Now, close your eyes again and think of someone who's passed, someone who's on the other side. This could be a family member, a friend, or someone else you knew. Open up your clairaudience—focus on the spot right above your physical ears. Allow the person to send you a song or music. Pay attention to the type of music that you hear. Was it a church choir? Was it a big band? Was it a song from the radio, or was it somebody playing the piano? Were they singing to you? Perhaps it was even somebody playing the bagpipes.

Don't worry if you don't hear anything right away. Just keep your clairaudience open at least a full five

minutes to give it time. If you still don't hear anything, try again. You may finally hear a song from
your memory of them, and that is fine, too. For this
exercise, you are trying to become familiar with and
recognize the music that makes you think of that particular person.

When you feel you are done, try it again with
somebody else. Think of a different loved one who's
passed or another person that you'd like to be able
to recognize. Go ahead and think about them and
allow your clairaudience to open up and tune in to
whatever song or music relates to that particular
person.

When you are all done, open your eyes and write
everything down in your journal. How did it feel to
you? Did it feel good? Was it easy? Was it difficult?
Did you enjoy this exercise? Were you able to recognize the music? Did you even hear the music?

Feel free to go back and try this exercise anytime.
Remember, you need to do what feels good to you,
what feels right, even if it feels difficult at the time.

His Name Was What?

Hearing music is not the only way to experience clairaudience. Those voices inside your head may be real. It might
be time for you to stop shaking off the feeling that you are
crazy and instead embrace it. The voices you hear are not
always your imagination. But just like with your clairvoyant
abilities, you need to practice your clairaudience to be able
to recognize the sounds and words as well.

Often during our normal, everyday interactions, we don't enunciate our vocabulary. We have a tendency to talk quicker and sloppier because we're comfortable and relaxed. Interestingly enough, when we receive clairaudience messages they too can sound underenunciated.

Imagine when your radio station isn't 100 percent tuned in. You end up hearing static and white noise in the foreground as well as the background. Trying to communicate with the other side is like this. You need to tune in and focus on the pronunciation of the words that are coming through. In order to hear what's being said, you need to be on the same frequency or wavelength. Our messengers from the other side are constantly trying to update and change the way they communicate with us. But one thing remains consistent—their desire to send us messages in a way that we can understand. They will send us words that we're familiar with, and they will try and make it as simple as possible.

Years ago, I was with some friends at my sister's house. We were hanging out and talking about our upcoming books, as we are all authors. We began discussing how psychic ability exists and how to tune in to our intuition. Lynn took it a step further and asked for an off-the-cuff reading.

"Do you get anything about me?" asked Lynn.

"I see you are going to write a ton of books," my sister, Tammy, replied.

"Oh that's great!" Lynn replied. "How about you, Melanie? Do you get anything?"

"I'm hearing that Tammy is right. You've got a lot of books coming out. You're channeling them right on through and that's not going to slow down anytime soon," I answered.

"Oh, that's awesome! That's exactly what it feels like. It's as if I have to get them out as quickly as possible. Who do you think is giving you this information, Melanie?" asked Lynn.

"I'm not really sure. I keep hearing Herman, but I also hear an *F*," I responded, not quite sure exactly what it was I was getting.

Lynn began laughing, almost hysterically. She thought it was the funniest thing. I, however, wasn't too sure what was happening. I couldn't quite figure out if she was laughing at me or at something I had said. So of course I had to ask her.

"What is going on? What is so funny?"

"Oh, sorry. I am not laughing at you, I'm laughing at your confusion. You are actually 100 percent accurate. I totally understand the name you're trying to hear. It's my grandfather trying to come through," Lynn exclaimed.

"Okay, was his name Herman? Why am I getting an *F*?"

"His name was Ferman! That's why it was so funny! I'm sure you've never heard *that* name before!" Lynn replied, amazed.

This is a common form of clairaudience—hearing words or parts of words. Ferman sent me his name in a way I could interpret, or rather Lynn could interpret. I knew it was relevant, but I had no idea why I was hearing what I did until she translated it for me. When you are tuning in to your psychic hearing, it may seem as though your radio station is kind of fuzzy. Just keep adjusting your antenna and eventually you will hear things more clearly. This is not to say that every time you receive a clairaudient message you will understand it fully—you may not. But it does mean you will sharpen your reception a bit.

Being able to hear sounds not audible to your physical ears can take practice. Not everyone is born with this inherent psychic ability. For some of you, however, it may be your strength. Either way, working on your physical hearing helps to improve your understanding of clairaudient messages because it affords you the opportunity to decipher the words you are listening to on this plane before trying to perceive them from the other side.

Exercise: Do You Hear the Words That Are Coming Out of My Mouth?

For this exercise, you should be prepared to go somewhere. Go to the mall, the park, a restaurant, or a coffee shop where you can sit and listen. You need to go where people are talking, so steer clear of the library!

Normally, we try and tune out conversations and ignore them if we know they don't pertain to us or our life. This time, you are going to try and tune in to the words and train your brain to hear physically with much more clarity than you've ever attempted before.

Sit where you are comfortable and don't worry about looking out of sorts. If necessary, give yourself a prop or two by opening your journal and bowing your head so no one will notice you. Then, take five long, deep breaths and close your eyes.

Let yourself hear the chatter all around you. Ideally, you should've picked a place that is densely populated so you have to really listen. Start off with an easy conversation. Pick someone who is sitting next to you at the closest table. Really focus on what the person is saying.

Can you hear her/his words? Are you able to make them out clearly? Listen for at least a few minutes to get your mind focused in and then switch it up. Eavesdrop on someone else's conversation and continue doing this with people who are farther and farther away from you. Be sure to really task yourself to meet the challenge and snoop on conversations that are happening a great distance away. The more difficult, the better.

While eavesdropping is not something you should normally try to excel at, practicing it for the sake of helping your clairaudient abilities is perfectly acceptable. (At least I think so!) The better you become at listening and deciphering with your physical ears the words that people are saying, the more apt you will be to recognize the words that are sent to you clairaudiently.

Hearing Sounds

Hearing music or words is not the only way to experience clairaudience; hearing sounds is common as well. Think about how many unique sounds there are in the world. On any given day you may hear birds singing, children laughing, cars driving, computer keys typing, people walking, dogs barking, machines moving, garbage trucks grinding, and even sirens whistling. While each is its own sound, there is uniqueness within the resonance itself. For example, there are a variety of sirens for fire trucks and police cars. Every child's laugh, though sharing the common theme of happiness, will have its own pitch. Each species of bird has a special tune, and all machines are different.

The sounds that are present in your physical world are also there to be utilized in your psychic world. Your clairaudient receptors, if you will, are able to recognize sounds because they are similar and at times even the same as the ones we hear with our physical ears. Distinguishing the sounds you hear externally or with your outer ear versus the sounds you hear psychically or with your inner ear can be a challenge. With practice, however, you'll soon discover a whole world of exquisite noise and chatter. The cacophony of noise will become discernible, and you will be awarded with true psychic hearing.

I had a woman who traveled across the country from California to Connecticut to come in for a reading. During her session, she told me she needed to hear everything I was getting.

"There are many things I want to know about, but I want to see what you pick up," Marjorie told me.

"I'm hearing something that sounds like chatter," I told her. "I'm also hearing a hammer or something. It almost seems like a judge's gavel striking down. Does that make sense to you?"

"It makes perfect sense," she replied with a smirk.

"Hmmm. The chatter sounds kind of angry. I'm hearing something about your husband. Did he pass and leave you with nothing?" I continued.

"He did indeed! That son of a bitch! He's miserable even after he died!" she exclaimed.

"Oh, I'm so sorry. That's too bad. But I'm also hearing another hum. This time it feels more happy. It's almost as if I'm in a kennel or something because it sounds like a bunch of dogs barking and yipping all at once? I get the feeling that some are alive and some have passed? I'm also hearing the name Henry, though I can't tell if that was for your husband or your dog!" I laughed.

Marjorie laughed, too! After her miserable husband died, she got a new dog to add to her other two. She named him Henry after her late spouse thinking she'd at least be able to take her frustration out on her husband by yelling at her dog. What happened, however, as she explained to me, was she ended up loving the dog, wholly, and it changed the way she felt toward Henry, the expired human version. Hearing that I was able to hear the ruckus of all the dogs in her life, both alive and dead, made her day. They were a big part of how she had been able to cope with the loss of her husband.

In Marjorie's case, I heard, using my clairaudience, two very distinct sounds that meant everything to her. The judge's gavel helped her understand that her late husband was around, or at the very least he was somewhat apologetic for what he had done. He was able to share one of her most recent memories so I could relay it to her; the chatter of the courtroom. These identifying and distinct sounds helped her to process what had happened and to accept that I was connecting to the other side for her.

The other noise that came through, the barking dogs, brought her back from being sad, depressed, and even angry to being cheerful and showing outward joy. She loved her dogs and treated them as part of her family. They gave her the unconditional love she felt her husband denied her after he passed and helped her to know that, again, the other side was busy sending her happiness that she could appreciate.

Both of these messages came through loud and clear, channeled by me for her. They validated what she was feeling and allowed her to process her emotions swiftly, leaving her with the delight she felt with her canine companions as opposed to the misery she had been experiencing regarding her deceased husband. By trusting what I was psychically hearing, with my internal ears, I was able to share some very important information with Marjorie, all through the recognition of a couple of seemingly random sounds. If I had discounted what I heard, I never would have been able to bring that joy to her that, I learned later on, was a precursor to moving past having been slighted in Henry's will.

It's so very important to understand the sounds that you hear with your physical ears. In order to process any clairaudient noise, you need to discern what it is you may be listening to. That means sound recognition. Deciphering the sounds makes them familiar to you so you're able to perceive them when they are sent to you psychically.

Exercise: Sounds Like …

As with the previous exercise, you need to be present in the real world with activities around you. Take yourself out to eat or to the mall. Be outside in the city or even wander through a home improvement warehouse store. What you are looking for is somewhere there are many different sounds.

Now begin listening, and I mean really listening, to the noise around you. If you are inside a restaurant or café, you may hear sounds of people talking as well as utensils hitting plates. Once you become really tuned in, you might even hear the subtle sound of ice cubes melting and moving in a glass. Don't just scan the room; listen to each distinct reverberation until you're sure you are able to identify it and what it sounds like.

In your journal, write down all of the different noises you are tuning in to and recognizing. When you feel you've completely heard every sound there is to decipher in that particular location, move on to the next place. Make a day of it. When you are all through, you may have well over a hundred different discernible noises or noise patterns recorded in your journal. These are crucial in interpreting messages you receive using your clairaudient sense.

My Ears Are Where?

For the most part, up until now, you've been using your physical hearing, one of your commonly utilized five senses. But to truly use your psychic ears, you need to tune in to your clairaudience. The chakra that helps you tap into this amazing psychic ability is not in the same spot your external ears are. Rather, the fifth chakra, or communication chakra, is located in your throat area and is responsible for your ability to relay messages using your voice as well as take delivery of messages with your clairaudience.

This throat chakra can be tricky. Because it is connected to your clear communication, it plays a big role in not only psychically hearing but also channeling what's being sent to you. If there are any physical problems in the throat area, this can block the clairaudient messages from being understood. Sore throats or even thyroid issues can make it more difficult to tune in.

Acknowledging the voices you are hearing in your head can be difficult. It can be increasingly difficult because you are not experiencing the sounds through your physical ears, which may make it feel as though you are inventing the messages. Knowing the communication is really channeling through your throat somehow makes it easier to swallow—no pun intended! Learning how to access that chakra will help you receive and interpret the messages you hear with your clairaudience.

Exercise: Why So Blue?

Tuning in to your fifth or communication chakra is easy, now that you've located it. You need to go somewhere quiet where you won't be disturbed. Then relax. Get really, really comfortable. Position yourself so your neck is somewhat stretched out and open.

Now, breathe. Inhale. Exhale. Pay attention to how your throat feels as you continue to breathe in and out deeply. When you inhale, imagine breathing in a beautiful blue light and let that light travel into your neck and swirl all over and through it. On the exhalation, imagine every other color leaving your neck and throat area, taking with it any negativity or negative energy that's been sitting there. Allow your breath to get rid of anything that no longer suits you or that's been stuck in your throat.

As you continue to bring the blue light into your neck and pass the other colors out, imagine a spinning wheel in your throat. It may look like an old record turning without a turntable, or it may even resemble a pinwheel. Imagine now that the blue light is filling up that disk, making it the most brilliant color conceivable.

Allow this chakra to continue spinning—stronger, faster, bluer, and more clearly than ever before. Focus on this area and feel the warmth that spreads throughout it. This is your communication chakra, your clairaudient center, and it's now open and ready to be used.

Acknowledge Me!

Sometimes it's not just about acknowledging the voices you are hearing for yourself. Often, it's about the client or friend understanding the message you are receiving for them. This can be difficult if it's an unexpected communication.

More often than not, when clients come to my office for a reading they are not only looking for guidance in their personal life, they are also hoping to connect to someone who has passed on. Inevitably, they have almost a preprogrammed idea of who is going to come through, essentially based only on their own desire to communicate with that particular person. For the most part, this is great, as usually the one they want to talk with does make an appearance in some way and having the client reach out to them ahead of time can help to bring their energy closer, making it easier for me to connect. But often, other loved ones, maybe even twice removed, want to come through and clients are unable to acknowledge them because they are so focused on the other friends or relatives they can't even think straight. Or we tune in with someone and after that the only people the clients can imagine are those possibly connected to the initial spirit that came through. Such was the case when my client Mary came in.

"I'm getting a bad headache and I'm hearing *J*, either the letter or the name. I feel like there is something wrong with this young man's head. I'm feeling an impact of some sort with my clairsentience (see chapter 4). I'm also hearing a car accident or something because I can hear the sound of breaking glass and a big impact. Strangely enough, he's also telling me to say, 'You're the president!' Does any of this make sense to you?" I asked Mary.

"Wow. I think so!" she replied. She went on to explain that her daughter's friend Jason (*J* name) had recently passed from a car accident during which he had flown out of the window, breaking it on impact, and landed on his head, causing him to die.

"Okay, well, what's the 'You're the president!' thing?" I continued.

"Before he died they were playing a game and she was sitting on his lap. I'm not sure exactly what the game was, but it had to do with someone being named the 'president.' I can't believe it," she shared.

"Be sure to tell her he says hello!" I relayed. "I'm also hearing a name that sounds like 'Coe' or 'Chlo' or something like that. Does this make sense to you?"

"No. I don't know what that means. It's not his last name and he didn't have a company or anything that would be Coe. I really don't know," Mary responded.

"Hmmm," I continued, feeling like it was significant in some way. "I'm still hearing Coe or Chlo?"

"I really don't understand that."

"It doesn't have to be related to Jason. It's a woman, and she is insisting I keep going until you get it," I told her, sure that it was a loved one coming through.

"Are you sure it's not a different name? It doesn't make sense to me," Mary reiterated.

"I'm positive. She's yelling at me now. 'Tell her Chlo!' she keeps saying. I'm sorry, but I'm not getting anything else with it other than she's older."

I know if someone from the other side keeps coming at me with information, I have to keep giving it to my client. I could feel the spirit energy getting a bit agitated that they weren't being acknowledged, so I continued.

"One more time, she wants me to tell you her name began with or sounded like Coe or Chlo. She's not giving up."

"I don't know what to tell you, I really don't—" and Mary was cut off mid-sentence by the impact of my cell phone hitting the wall.

"What the—?" we both said at the same time.

My phone, which had been sitting on my desk, had flown off into the wall.

"Oh my God! What just happened? You must've had it on vibrate, right?" Mary asked, grasping for an explanation.

"No, it was totally turned off. Still is, as a matter of fact. Chlo says she did it!"

"It's Chlotilde! My grandmother!" Mary exclaimed. The impact of the phone hitting had jarred her consciousness and allowed her to move beyond Jason and kind of regroup. In her defense, as it turns out, they usually called her Tillie instead of Chlotilde.

"Well, that explains the *T* name I also wrote down!" I laughed. "She wants you to let your mother know she loves her and she's more than worthy and she apologizes for not recognizing that more when she was here." Now that Mary had acknowledged her grandmother, I was able to deliver this important message.

A year passed and Mary came back for another reading.

"Tillie's here. Do you understand that?" I asked her. I never remember readings and especially don't recall loved ones who come through for people. Sometimes I feel like it makes everything flow and keeps me less cluttered, but other times it seems it would be providential to be able to pull up from memory the deceased loved ones I've already connected to for my clients.

"Yes, of course. That's my grandmother; the same one who sent your phone flying across the room last year!" Mary replied with a giggle.

"Oh! I don't remember that! Anyway, she wants to tell you that you need to tell your mother what she told you last time!"

"Oh my ... I was going to tell my mother, but I thought it would make her way too upset, so I never passed on the message," she admitted, a bit nervous.

This time, Mary went home and shared the message with her mom. It was in that moment she realized what a special gift it was—one her mother had apparently waited her whole life to hear. After coming to me for about six years now, she admits that anytime I tell her to pass anything on to someone, she immediately does. After all, the people on the other side have a broader understanding of what's happening here and what we need. There is no denying that anymore for Mary.

Exercise: Remember Me

For this exercise it is crucial you get out a pen and your journal. Write down everyone you have ever been connected to who has passed. Include deceased loved ones in your family as well as friends and even coworkers. Go all the way back to when you were a baby, and then keep going! Often, we decide just because we never met our grandfather he won't come through. Not true. They are your relatives, not to mention you have their bloodline. You are absolutely connected, so don't discount them.

Next, ask family members and friends questions about the people you've added to your list. Include names, dates, locations, physical attributes, etc. Gather as much information on each person as you can. Include any pets you had that have passed. They are part of your family as well.

Once you're sure you have a pretty comprehensive list, sit down somewhere quiet and practice your protection meditation. Then, open up your communication chakra and your clairaudience by focusing on the color blue flowing through and around your neck and throat area. Do this for about five minutes.

Then listen. That's right, simply listen. Allow any sounds, voices, names, initials, or messages to come through. Ask who is there and what they want to share with you. If they don't answer right away, ask again. Then wait. Give it at least five minutes if you still don't hear anything. Keep asking for any type of information, but be sure to tell them only positive energy is allowed to come through. You don't want to communicate with anything other than energies with the highest frequencies.

When you feel you've received everything there is at this time, open your eyes and write it all down. Does it make sense? Do you understand what they told you? Do you know who shared the information? Was it someone from your list? Do you need to relay any messages to anyone else? Remember, as with

Mary, don't judge or censor what comes through. Your job is just to be the open channel.

Make a note of how it felt to use your clairaudience to connect to the other side. Did it feel right? Did it feel comfortable? Uncomfortable? Easy? Difficult? Write it all down and appreciate and validate the energies that worked hard to get you the messages!

four

Clairsentience
(Clear Feeling or Clear Sensing)
& Clairempathy (Clear Emotion)

*"Acting on your psychic feelings is the leap of faith that will
propel you forward into the world of the extraordinary."*

—SONIA CHOQUETTE

We are all sensitive; we just may not realize it. Being sensitive means we are able to pick up the subtle energies that are around us. Clairsentient abilities are one of the most under-recognized and undervalued gifts we possess. Not because it's not awesome to be able to feel things psychically, but because we use it so often it becomes almost second nature and we don't always comprehend that we are accessing our clear feeling.

"Many of us are unconscious or unaware sensitives, picking up quantities of subliminal information and ideas that remain just below the surface of our conscious minds without knowing what we're doing," said prominent author and intuitive Penney Peirce. (Peirce, 2009)

Clairsentience is probably the most commonly utilized psychic sense. Clairsentience is also the most disregarded psychic sense. We use this ability without even realizing it. Many of us pick up and feel what others are going through, otherwise known as empathy. Still more of us have gut feelings or instincts regularly. The key to utilizing these clairsentient vibes, these psychic feelings, is simply to begin recognizing them.

We can physically feel when we cut our finger or when we fall down. We can appreciate how it feels when we are personally excited about something. We can sympathize with someone who is grieving. We, quite easily, can feel when we are hungry because we are able to physically interpret the growling in our stomachs. We also have the ability to long for something, or recognize when there is something missing from our lives that we desire with our mental and emotional states of mind. We distinguish these sensations through the use of our normal, everyday senses. Clairsentience, though it may expose the same types of feelings or emotions, is about feeling with our sixth sense.

Clairempathy

I can't stand when I feel aggravated seemingly without reason. It's that mood that just doesn't fit and is hard to justify. When there is cause to feel aggravated it makes sense, but when there's not, it leaves you feeling like something is all kinds of wrong. Anyone with teenagers can tell you this irritated state of mind can occur without warning, as can deep or even fleeting immense passion.

There's a reason for this sensation of being frustrated or feeling out of control of your own emotions. Sometimes, of course, it's normal, all part of the everyday fluctuating current. However, quite often it's because of clairsentience or clairempathy. Many of us who experience clairsentient ability will also possess empathic gifts, or the ability to take on the feelings of others. These empathic emotions can include aggravation that stems from someone else's feelings. Once you realize the source is not internal, but rather external, it becomes easier to settle the brewing irritation down.

My daughter Molly, whom I love with all my heart, is a teenager and goes through the typical adolescent struggles. As we all know, it's difficult to learn how to cope with those ups and downs (and I'm not just talking about her!). It is a process. Today, she was in one of those moods. Now, I'm not saying she did anything wrong. I'm just talking about a mood where I could literally feel the slogging angst and stress dripping off of her. Her energy was filled with discontent. Not that there was any reason she could pinpoint. She didn't do anything to me or even say anything negative for that matter. She was just there, saturated with annoyance.

When she's like this, I instantly pick up on it and have a difficult time shedding it until I know the root cause of what I have tapped into. I don't necessarily have to know what's wrong with her; I just have to discover that I'm picking up her energy, which is not always so easy to do. Once I understand the energy I'm feeling isn't mine, it becomes much easier to change it from negative to positive and feel uplifted and light again, which can have the added benefit of cheering her as well. Until then, well, let's just say I'm not the happiest person either.

Clairsentient, or more specifically clairempathic, abilities contribute to feeling good as well. Whenever I think of picking up on someone's happy energy, I think of over-the-top joy. I'm sure you can picture it, too. Imagine going to a friend's house and the person tells you, quite excitedly, that they just got a publishing deal for their new book. They begin jumping up and down, laughing out of sheer happiness, and grab your hands. In an instant, you are caught up in their intense emotion as well—screaming, laughing, and even crying right along with them. This is not because it's your book deal or because you will benefit in some way or even because you are so incredibly pleased for them. Rather, it's due to the fact that you are now in their energy, picking up on their incredibly heightened emotions. These are the fun ones, the emotions that soar you into the sky, floating you up on a cloud. These feelings can even release your endorphins, the chemicals inside your brain that make you feel elated.

The two examples above are extreme opposites, though they have something in common. Both involve empathetic senses or more specifically feeling what others are feeling. This is one form of clairsentience—the ability to pick up on the emotions or senses of others. This is known as clairempathy. People who have this type of clairsentient gift are able to both tune in to another's emotional state and take on another's emotions, which can bring extreme feelings ranging from misery to bliss or anything in between.

Because you are taking on the energy of someo
very important to protect yourself.

Exercise: More Than a Feeling

Keeping your own energy field safe from being taken over by someone else's is simple, but it is something we quite often forget to do. Before working with your empathic abilities be sure to invoke your protection from the introduction.

For this exercise, you are going to need a friend. Try and choose someone who you know is passionate about things. You want it to be a friend who regularly experiences life on a deeper level—someone who can just as easily laugh as cry.

Have your friend sit down, facing you, while you sit facing away from them. Then, have them think about some time in their life where they experienced intense emotion. It doesn't matter what that emotion was, it just has to be strong. Have them try and silently relive their feelings during that time or experience. For example, if it was the loss of a loved one, have them focus on how it made them feel rather than the actual person. If it was a celebration, ask them to recall the joy surrounding the event.

When you are both ready, allow yourself to sit still, letting the emotion of your partner begin to wash over you, filling you. Have them intentionally send the energy and the strength of their feelings to you by imagining a ribbon of energy flowing out of their chest into your back. Your job is to allow that energy to spread through you until you experience the emotion yourself.

After sitting for about five minutes in this state, share what you felt with your partner. Go into detail. Sometimes a single word can't describe fully the emotion you are feeling. For example, you may feel angst, but does that mean worry or fear or anger or frustration? Explain. Then, have them share what they were sending you. Were you close? Did you hit it dead on? Were you totally off? Try it again, having your partner remember a different event in their life.

After you've done it a few times, switch places. Are you a better receiver or sender? Is your friend able to pick up on or feel your emotions? Are there any emotions that felt stronger for either of you? Was joy easier to understand or was sadness? Go over how it worked for both of you, but don't over-analyze it. You may find that the more you practice, the better you become. Empathic abilities are more than just being sympathetically understanding to someone else's state of being. It may mean you are tuning in to your clairsentient awareness.

Why Do I Feel This Way?

Kids tend to take on the emotions of others without realizing they've tapped into someone else's feelings. This happens quite often with groups. Children have a tendency to want to fit in—let's be honest, we all do! It's easier sometimes to blend into a group, and those who are already predisposed to clairempathic gifts will take on the group's overall mood. These empathic impressions generally are not recognized for what they are unless they make us feel really uncomfortable or different. It's kind of what is known as the mob mentality (though not necessarily with a negative twist). What one feels, the next one feels, etc. The confusion comes from reacting with a negative slant, not feeling good, or not understanding where the feelings came from. "Why do I feel this way?" is quite often a question I get when I work with kids.

Now, granted, we all experience a wide range of emotions regularly. But with people who tend to be clairempathic, it's more prevalent. Those who are more sensitive to this form of clairsentience will have a harder time discerning their own feelings from someone else's. This happened with Claudia.

"I don't know why, but I keep feeling like someone's taking over my body or my brain or something! I feel all kinds of fuzzy inside," said my fourteen-year-old client.

"Tell me some more. When does this seem to happen?" I asked her.

"I guess when I'm listening to my friends talk. Is it because I don't care? Or because I don't want to hear it? I feel like I'm being a bad listener, but I get all freaked out and just kind of shut down because it feels like I'm sharing their experience," she continued.

"That's because you're empathic," I told Claudia. "You are taking on their emotions, which is why it feels so weird and freaks you out. It's not your stuff; it's theirs."

"That makes perfect sense! Wow! I get it now! So, is there anything I can do?" she implored.

"That's the good news. You can protect yourself so you don't have to take on everyone else's stuff."

I went on to teach Claudia how to protect herself by using the protective bubble of white light. When I saw her months later, she said she felt much better. She was a better listener, didn't feel weighed down, and felt like a better friend. She was much happier because she had learned to control her clairsentient gift, more specifically, her clairempathy.

Exercise: How Do I Feel?

Just like you did the last time, you are going to practice using your clairempathic gifts. Before you begin, you need to create a safeguard for yourself so you don't take on others' feelings.

Imagine a filter, much like an air filter for a car or even a coffee filter. Now, see in your mind that filter material stretching around you, encompassing you at a safe distance, but that it is see-through. That filter is now employed to keep out any unwanted emotions, while at the same time allowing the good stuff to trickle in so you are able to understand what others feel but not take on anyone else's emotions. Imagine that filter growing larger, stronger, and also more flexible so that it moves with you, keeping you protected and safe.

Once you're sure you've done that, take yourself somewhere you can be around other people. Don't tell them you are working your psychic abilities, but allow their emotions to strain through your filter. When you've picked up on their energy, then, and only then, ask them how they are doing. If you know them well, get deep. Ask them if they've been feeling anything or experiencing anything in particular. Does it match what you've picked up on? Is it different? Tell them the emotions you were feeling and ask them if they have merit. Do they? How does it feel to you to be able to empathically connect but stay protected at the same time?

Do You Feel What I Feel?

Empathic feeling is only one aspect of clairsentience. Clairsentience allows us to feel not just what others feel but also a wide variety of situations, people, locations, etc. Anything you can see, hear, or know you can clairsentiently feel as well. Now, this may seem strange; how can you feel people? It's simple. Trust your gut. It's really about sensing someone or something with your psychic ability rather than your five senses.

Law enforcement personnel talk about following their hunches or their gut instincts all the time. Psychotherapists assess situations with clients using their gut reactions to what they're being told to determine the validity of what their client is saying. Mothers respect their gut instincts when they feel something's off with their children. Your gut instincts are exactly what they sound like—feelings you have in your gut. These gut instincts, or clairsentient abilities, are closely related to the third, or solar plexus, chakra. This yellow energy center located in your abdomen helps you feel things on a visceral level and sends those feelings throughout your other extrasensory translators to enhance your understanding of what you are experiencing.

Gut instincts keep us safe. How many times have you instinctively dodged the proverbial bullet? We all have run our hands over our forehead while making the *phew* sound at least once in our lives because we listened to instincts that told us to stay away from a situation or a person and it turned out we were right to heed our own internal warning. We are all sensitive to our surroundings and our lives; it's just a matter of enhancing that sensitivity in order to increase our awareness of it.

The other day, I was driving home from my office. Basically, there are two different courses available. If I go one way, it means driving down a very narrow, steep, windy road, rock face on one side and cliff on the other. The other road involves turning off the main street and is straighter and flatter but a few minutes longer. For some reason it just seems easier to continue on the same road and traverse the somewhat dangerous path down.

That rainy day was no exception, yet as I passed the turnoff I began to feel a bit of tension developing in my body. I knew that was a sign that I needed to be extra careful, so I proceeded slowly, braking more often than normal. Before the next curve in the road, I had goose bumps and a feeling of dread. Immediately, even though there was a car practically riding on my rear bumper, I slowed to a crawl and almost stopped. As I came around the sharp corner, the cliff inches away on my right, I saw the cause of my apprehension. There was a huge moving truck taking up both lanes headed up the hill. The truck was so big it had no business being on this particular road, much less in the middle of it.

Luckily for both of us, I had listened to my intuition. My caution had afforded the driver of the truck time to move over just enough so that when we passed I was inches from his rear end. My life didn't flash before my eyes, but the goose bumps definitely took over my entire body. I realized I had been holding my breath the entire time. When I finally released the air from my body, I could clairsentiently feel the driver of the car that was tailgating me also let out a whoosh of relief. He backed off after that.

We tend to take these moments for granted—these little blips that occur, without warning or repetition, that we soon forget about. Most of us use this intuitive gift of clairsentience quite matter-of-factly, without always acknowledging what transpired. When these types of near accidents and moments of clear feeling happen, we focus more on the actual event than the intuitive vibe we got that kept us safe. For example, I told my daughter about what had happened simply because she is about to get her driver's license and I like to share little tidbits of information with her.

"But how did you know the truck was coming when you didn't see it?" Molly asked.

"I'm not sure. I had an uneasy feeling. I felt like there was something wrong, so I used my brakes," I replied, without really naming my intuition or the intuitive vibe I had gotten right before it happened.

"It's a good thing you're psychic," she replied honestly. "That just gave me goose bumps! That's validation that you used your psychic ability!"

All I could do was smile at her. She was right on.

Often these clairsentient abilities are developed early on when living in a dysfunctional family. Your instincts have to be honed almost to perfection to be able to survive the abusive alcoholic father by hiding before he comes home. Or those clairsentient feelings tune in to the untreated bipolar mother's tirade during her manic phase in order to protect your younger sibling and get them to safety. Or they develop to offset the isolation you felt in school when you had no one to talk to or share with so you spent a lot of time alone with only yourself for company. Clairsentience is developed as a means to protect yourself and those you love. Any of these situations, though not always necessarily as dire as those above, can segue into a clairsentient life; however, they are not a prerequisite to accessing your clear feeling.

This psychic sense can be used to avert potential problems, but this sensation is not always heeded. For instance, my client June shared one of her clairsentient forewarning stories with me.

"We were getting ready to go to a thirtieth birthday party with another couple and I just kept telling my husband I felt off, though I wasn't sure why. There was nothing physically going on and I didn't have any reason to be hesitant, but I was. I just didn't really want to go."

She went on to tell me that the vibe she had continued for a couple hours while she was there, actually at the party, and she just couldn't get comfortable. June couldn't describe it any other way except she felt off.

"I went downstairs next to the bar room and immediately knew why I'd been feeling that way. One of the guests, who was beyond inebriated, was starting a fight with my husband. Thank goodness my husband had enough sense to take himself out of the situation and leave so nothing escalated," she continued. "But that was enough to teach me that I need to listen to those feelings. That was definitely a clairsentient experience."

Living clairsentiently can help us, but it doesn't always feel comfortable. Take June's story for example. Here they were: her, her husband, and another couple. They were all ready to go to what promised to be a fun party. It certainly wouldn't have been right to back out or change plans at that point, though that's what her intuition was trying to tell her to do. Generally, it's simpler to go with the flow, even though going with the flow can mean going against your clairsentience. It then becomes a choice, and more often than not, the benefit of having made the tougher decision may not always be apparent. If June hadn't ignored her feeling and stopped everyone from going there is a good chance nothing would have happened at the party at all. Her husband wouldn't have been there, and there wouldn't have been a fight. If that had happened there wouldn't have been any validation that June made the right call. Luckily for her, it all turned out okay, though they won't be partying with that guest for quite a while. Next time, she said, she will try harder to understand what her clairsentience is trying to tell her so she can make a more informed decision, or at least be better prepared.

Gut instincts can also direct us to continue on a certain path or make a change—literally or figuratively. For example, I am terrible at direction. I get lost in the mall. My family makes fun of me, but I know it's just part of who I am. However, when I tune in and ask the universe to help me decide which way to go, I end up in the right direction. When I don't ask my guides or helpers, nine times out of ten I find myself at the complete opposite end from where I wanted to be. This happens to me a lot, at the mall and more importantly when trying to choose which path to take in my life. If I follow my instincts, I make out okay; if not, well let's just agree that it doesn't usually work out so well!

Exercise: Trust Your Gut

It's time to have a little fun. Take a few nice, deep breaths and allow yourself to relax. Tell the universe you'd like to "feel your way" using your gut instincts.

Now, get in your car. If you don't have a car, call a friend who's willing to spend an hour or so driving you or call a taxi (though it could get expensive) or even get on a bus or a train (no peeking at where you're going though!). You are going to drive to an area you are not familiar with and state your intention that you want to end up somewhere fun or at a great new place to eat or even somewhere to get ice cream. Be sure you make clear what you want before you begin driving.

Now, at every intersection ask your gut to direct which way you should go. Allow yourself enough time to travel to a location you've not been to before, but don't make it longer than an hour. At that point, you just would be trying to find something and it no longer would about allowing your intuition to guide you to your destination.

When you are done, assess how you made out. Did you make it to a location that qualifies as your goal? Were you close? Do you recognize where you are? Is it somewhere enjoyable?

You can try this for somewhere you know but have never been and don't know how to get to. Does it bring you there? Also, try it when house hunting. You may end up with your next new home! Put your kids in the mix; make a day of everyone taking turns deciding which direction to head in. This sometimes works out even better with young children because they generally don't know directions to anything outside of five minutes from their home.

Physical Signs of Clairsentience

Have you ever felt the hair on the back of your neck stand up? Or seemingly out of the blue be overtaken by goose bumps? What are goose bumps, really? These physical reactions are actually clairsentient manifestations of spirit presence. This type of response to paranormal activity is quite common and one of the most painless ways to experience clear feeling. It lets you know the energy has shifted around you. Feeling a heaviness or the opposite, a light and airy feeling, can demonstrate to you if something is negative or positive. Feeling something is dark versus light or vice versa will also assist you in interpreting between negative and positive aspects of whatever spirit, presence, or situation you are tuning in to.

Usually during sessions, I begin with my clairsentience. I allow my body to open to the universe and feel whatever I need to in order to give my clients the best possible reading. Sometimes, it will tell me what kind of mood they're going to be in when they walk through the door. Other times, it leads me to an answer for whatever question they may have. And more often than not, as Molly said about the truck and as I explain to my clientele, when I get goose bumps it validates that the information I'm sharing with my sitter is true and accurate or that spirit from the other side is trying to come through. I rely heavily on my clairsentient abilities.

Getting goose bumps—that prickly sensation that usually begins on the arms but can take over your head—your legs, and then some, can be an awesome experience. Marla understood just how incredible it could be during her recent reading with me.

"What is with the dog/dogs?" I asked her during her reading. Marla had come in hoping to validate that her mother was aware of what she was currently doing in her life from the other side, after having recently passed.

"I'm hearing 'It's a whole new experience!' and I keep feeling like the dogs are jumping on me. Do you identify with what I'm saying?" I continued.

I should have known by the tears welling up in her eyes that, yes, she got it.

"Yes. We inherited my mom's dog and our dog is not really liking the new situation!" she replied. "That is one of the questions I had for you today. I wanted to know if my mother knew we took her dog!"

"She absolutely is acknowledging it! Is her dog's name Daisy or Ditzy or something?" I asked.

"It's Dixie," she responded, and in that moment we both held up our arms.

"Goose bumps. They are confirmation that she's here and knows what we're talking about. And she's happy you have Dixie!" I told Marla.

The tears she had were a mixture of joy that her mother was aware and relief that she had done the right thing by bringing the dog in, even though there was some tension between the two canines now at the house. The goose bumps helped to physically corroborate that Mom was around and approved.

Most of my clients, upon receiving evidence their deceased loved ones are present, will experience some form of confirmation themselves. Frequently, this will show up in the most common form—goose bumps. More often than not, this prickly sensation will create a stir from the sitter, as they are not usually expecting to feel something like that.

This happened during another session with my client Arlene. We were about halfway through the reading when her mother was coming through. We had already accepted her presence, as she was very pointedly acknowledging family members and key situations in Arlene's life. But what she communicated to me next made the goose bumps practically jump off of both of us, head to toe.

"She wants to know if you found the rings," I shared with my client.

"Oh my God! I can't believe you just asked me that!" she laughed and cried at the same time.

"I'm feeling like she was a little funny or tricky with the rings. I'm also getting like you found them in the nick of time," I told her, smiling.

"You are absolutely right! We almost threw them out. We had no idea they were hidden away," she exclaimed.

"Okay, well now I really need to know. Where were they? I can feel her laughter."

"She had them in an old panty liner bag in the back of a drawer. We had just cleaned out that dresser and we were about to put everything in the garbage. For some reason, we checked and there they were!"

The goose bumps were out in full force. Those, added to the feeling of excitement my client had, completed her experience.

"This was the one question I had: I wanted to know if she was the reason we hesitated and didn't throw the bag away. Now I know. Awesome."

Exercise: Goose Bumps or Something Else?

Think back to the last time you experienced goose bumps or even some other type of similar sensation somewhere on or throughout your body. What were you doing? Where were you? What was going on around you? Did you feel different? Did you notice that you had them? Did you attribute the feeling to something paranormal or clairsentient? Did you just think it was from being chilled? How did it feel to have goose bumps or the shivers? Did it feel familiar? Was it a new sensation? Did you question their existence? Did you tell someone? Did you share what you were feeling? Did it change the way you thought? Did it change your beliefs? Did it feel like an intuitive vibe? Did it feel like clairsentience?

Write down all your answers and review them afterward. Was it the first time you ever felt that way? Do you think you will experience clairsentience in this way again?

Feeling Pulled

You've discovered how empathy is connected to clairsentience and how you may experience physical sensations like goose bumps. You've also learned that the rumbling in your belly may very well be more than the lunch you just had. Clairsentience is plainly and simply about clearly feeling something or having a feeling regarding something and, more importantly, noticing these feelings. There is no limit to what you can discover through clairsentience.

This psychic ability can help you with the location of a new home or job and a career choice as well. Certain areas on Earth may hold specific feelings for you, through your psychic senses. You may get a warm sensation when you think of Minnesota because your best friend lives there, or you may feel happy when you think of Florida because you have memories of visiting your grandparents there. New York City may stir excitement in your belly because of the last amazing play you saw there, and Connecticut may remind you of home because you grew up there. Paris may evoke feelings of love because that's where your husband proposed to you, and Italy may stir feelings of nostalgia for a time you spent there during college. Geographical areas can stir up your vibes, giving you clairsentient knowledge that you can utilize for many reasons.

My client Susan reminded me of how well my clairsentient abilities had worked for her daughter.

"You did a reading for my husband a few years ago. He asked you about our daughter and what you got for her regarding work."

Now, as a rule, I don't remember readings, especially one from a few years previous. So, I told Susan this.

"That's okay because we remember it! You told him you felt her working in Westport, and we didn't believe you," she laughed.

She went on to explain that I had told Bob, her husband, that I felt pulled to the Sound, a part of the ocean that bordered Connecticut and Long Island. I told him I specifically felt drawn to the waterfront town of Westport.

Susan took it even further. "Then, our daughter came in for her own reading. She asked you what you felt she would be doing for work and you told her you were feeling she would be doing something physical, with her body. You could feel her body moving and stretching."

What made this even more interesting was Devon, the young lady we were talking about, was graduating from college with a history degree. There was no physically demanding career in her future that she could fathom at all.

"Hmmm. So, did my clairsentience pay off? Does this now make sense?" I asked Susan, unsure of what her response or the outcome would be.

"It actually makes perfect sense. Devon is now a certified yoga instructor and teaches in Westport. You were right on the money."

It wasn't that I saw where she would be or what she would be doing. I didn't hear the words "yoga" and "Westport." I felt them, clairsentiently, based on my knowledge of the area and the feeling I had throughout my body. Taking notice of the sensations you have can be the catalyst to connecting to your own intuition and your psychic senses.

Exercise: Where Are You?

Take some paper or blank cards and write the names of locations you've been or that you have feelings about. Use one card per place. When you have at least ten different cards/locations, shuffle them and put them in a bag or a hat.

Take a nice deep breath. Allow your body to relax, beginning with your toes. Feel that relaxation traveling up through your calves and your shins, through your knees and your thighs. Allow it to continue moving up into your reproductive area and your hips, your abdomen, and your solar plexus. Feel that relaxation move into your chest and through your shoulders, out your arms and your elbows and your wrists, trickling out through your hands and your fingertips. On the next deep breath, feel it flowing through your throat and neck and into your jaw muscles. Allow it to travel into your cheeks and your eyes and your forehead, relaxing every muscle as it moves up. Feel the energy of that relaxation travel out the top of your head and flow down, over, and around your body.

Once you feel completely relaxed, take the bag or hat with the locations and pick a card without looking at it. Lie down and place it on your solar plexus. Try and determine which location it is by how it feels in your body and which direction it pulls you in. After you've spent a few minutes on it, look at the card. Did you get it right? If so, great! Do it again! If not, that's okay. You still have plenty of others to try it with!

What the Truth Holds

I teach intuitive development regularly. Whether it be one-on-one or with groups, most people who come to me have an incredible desire to tune in to their psychic senses but feel uncontrollably stagnant in that area. I don't try and convince them they are psychic or even intuitive. I am just the conduit to helping their own natural gifts become more present.

The process can be a lot of fun, but for the person trying to tap into their abilities it can also be discouraging at times. Think about working out. If you haven't been exercising your specific muscles, it can be very difficult to try and use them, let alone be able to flex them and have them feel solid and strong. You need to focus on each particular muscle group to truly create a better physique. It's the same with your psychic muscles. Imagine these psychic senses are muscles that have to be worked out. If you haven't been strengthening them, it'll absolutely be more difficult to get them to flex or do what you want them to do.

My client Sandy had been coming to me for about a month. She knew she had some type of intuitive vibes but couldn't quite grasp exactly how she was receiving information. She had decided she really wanted to work on developing this talent. She believed her greatest potential was in clairaudience or even clairvoyance, so we started there. I knew she was gifted with clairsentience, as most people are, but I also knew it would be advantageous to work on awakening all of her senses.

We began by opening up her clairvoyance. I put three different envelopes in front of her and let her pick which she wanted to psychically tune in to. Inside were three different things. One held a menu, one held a picture of a deceased loved one, and one held a picture of animals. Each was different and afforded her the opportunity to stretch her psychic vision. After we did this exercise, she declared she was not quite in tune with her clairvoyance. We then moved on to her clairaudience using the same technique. Again she felt a disconnect.

I asked her to try something else, as I knew she had a natural clairsentient ability. I needed her to feel it within her body. This time, I had her venture into mediumship. I asked her to look at a photo. Next, I instructed her to tune in to the sensations she felt in her body.

"Do you feel light and airy? Does it feel like you are full of life?"

"I'm not really sure," Sandy responded with a perplexed look on her face.

"Do you feel heavy? Is it harder to breathe than normal?" I continued.

"Yes, it is. What does that mean?" she asked.

"You tell me. Do you feel the person in the picture is alive? Or has she passed?"

"Well, based on how it feels in my body I'd have to say she's passed," she said. "Do you know if that's true?"

It was true. She was holding a picture of my mother, who had unfortunately passed a few years previously. I was able to confirm that she was correct. I took it a step further and had her feel in her body how my mom had died.

"I'm not positive, but did she have problems with her lungs? Also, I'm feeling heaviness in her legs. I'm actually feeling like it's some type of systemic thing, maybe throughout her entire body."

She was right. My mother died from complications with lupus. At the end of her life, she had a very difficult time breathing and her legs were so swollen they were rupturing. Sandy was definitely tuning in to her clairsentient abilities.

Exercise: Dead or Alive?

Ask a friend or a handful of friends to come play with you. All of you need to gather together photographs of people both dead and alive. Turn them all over (be sure to cross out or tape over anything written on the backs) and mix them all up together. Separate them and line them up in a row.

Invoke your circle of protection and breathe energy into your solar plexus. Feel the rise and fall as you inhale positive energy and exhale any negative debris. Imagine your power center expanding, spreading out toward the pictures.

Slide a picture out of the row toward you. Don't hold it, but begin to pay attention to how it feels. Does it make you feel alive? Does it cause you to be tired? Are you feeling healthy? Or sick? Without questioning it just say out loud everything you feel.

Continue on by sharing if the person in the photograph is male or female, young or old, etc. Feel it, don't see it. Let your gut tell you the answers without judgment, reservation, or scrutiny. Speak what you know.

When you are done, turn over the photograph. You should be able to see whether some of what you tuned in to is correct or not. Have whoever supplied the picture chime in with their validations. Were you on? Were you off? Were you close?

Have each of your friends take a turn reading the pictures. How do the others do? Are they able to tune in? Compare notes. Take advantage of like-minded friends who enjoy playing in your psychic arena and do this exercise often. You may find your hits begin to outweigh your misses as your clairsentience develops.

Baby, You Were Born This Way

I had an interesting experience the other day. I was in my daughter's school for a sports meeting with a bunch of students and parents. We had casually broken up into groups; adults sitting together, children sitting together. I had three different people who were already seated ask me to sit next to them. It didn't feel right, though I didn't know why at the time. Instead, I decided to pull up a chair with my back to the front of the room (something I normally would never do) and join a group that way. We chatted for a bit until the meeting started and the coach began speaking. Turns out, she was standing in the back of the classroom instead, so I was facing her. At that point, I decided I'd figured out why I wanted to sit there.

As she was talking, we were all listening. It was a very comfortable atmosphere, a bit of joking and happy energy. I felt glad to be there. Then it hit me. I was directly in front of a board where she had posted vocabulary words and their basic one-word meanings. Simple words like "rival = opposing," "precise = exact," etc. One stood out to me and, to be honest, caught me off-guard. It had me pondering it, while at the same time I felt an overwhelming sense of delight. It was "intuition." She could have written just about anything as the meaning, but what she wrote gave me hope and filled me with awe. "Intuition = natural." My seventh grader's teacher was teaching that intuition was natural. I was blown away and very excited to see this. Granted, I may have read more into it than was necessary, but I was very happy. Intuition *is* natural, and it was wonderful to see it so innocently stated.

We all have the ability to feel things, whether we label it clairsentience or not. This incredible gift is a normal and, yes, a natural part of life. Our clairsentient senses, our intuition, are crucial in recognizing and understanding what best serves us and what feels good. We are, indeed, lucky to be given such a gift.

five

Claircognizance (Clear Knowing)

"I don't know how I know what I know,
I just know that I know it."

—CHIP COFFEY

Sometimes you just know things, without even knowing how or why you know it. This is claircognizance, and every one of us will experience this at least once in our lifetime. It can be the coolest, most miraculous form of psychic ability but is often the most overlooked.

"So, when will I get the next check?" my client Sven asked. He's a contractor, and like so many he is living hand to mouth, or paycheck to paycheck.

"You will get something on Tuesday and something on Thursday," I responded without hesitation.

"How do you know that?" he continued with a questioning look.

"I just know. Mark my words. You will get two checks—one on Tuesday and one on Thursday," I repeated.

Sure enough, he received two checks that week on those specific days. It wasn't that I saw a calendar in my mind or that I heard the days spelled out. I just knew the answer instantly by tapping into my claircognizant psychic sense.

Psychic ability is about perceiving that which is not readily accessible or available using only the five physical senses. Claircognizance takes those physical senses and throws them out the window. Without rhyme or reason this incredible psychic sense takes you to a plane of existence that leaves you wondering, "How the heck did I know that?" If you want to develop your psychic senses, you need to train your awareness.

Your seventh chakra, the crown chakra, is located on the very top of your head. It is where your spontaneous knowing or claircognizance is centered. It is where you are spiritually connected to the universe and even where deceased loved ones and your guides can easily influence your ideas and thoughts. It is this chakra that connects you to the spirit world, opening much like a floodgate on a dam to allow information to flow through to you.

Tuning in to your crown chakra creates the opportunity needed to activate your claircognizant sense. Sometimes this happens quite easily and even matter-of-factly. Other times it takes a conscious effort to really turn on this incredible sense. It goes beyond most rational processes to believing we can just know something that we have no logical basis in knowing. Yet, this is how claircognizance works.

Meditation is a gateway to opening up those ps senses. It is an important tool in developing your intuiti and one that shouldn't be overlooked. By meditating, you allow your mind, body, and spirit to slow down and relax, becoming more open and, yes, even vulnerable, to channeling information that is right there in the universe, ready to be tapped into. Sometimes people have a hard time slowing down enough and getting out of their own way to feel they can successfully meditate. I am one of those people. I have a hard time shutting down my own mind chatter. Even still, utilizing every tool in your toolbox is the most productive avenue to strengthening those muscles and learning to flex them.

Meditation is a huge part of spirituality and a great way to access your claircognitive gifts. It is not just an Eastern practice or even a religious exercise. Meditation's history extends all the way back to prehistoric times when rhythmic chants were practiced to appease the gods and bring food, health, and shelter. Practicing meditation spans the globe, with roots in Hinduism, Taoism, Buddhism, Islam, and even Christianity to name a few. Meditation is not limited to one religion or one race; instead it crosses every boundary to bring peace, relaxation, and focus to all. It is an unbiased, nonprejudiced nonreligion.

Lao Tzu, the unofficial father of Taoism, stated, "To the mind that is still, the whole universe surrenders." Meditation, at its core, is a form of relaxation where the mind is cleared through conscious focus, and therefore creates a state of conscious and unconscious awareness as an end to itself or to realize some benefit. It is a tool that can be used to garner

ı and feelings of peace, love, joy, and
ılso bring you to a state of heightened
ıting a vibrational level that will pro-
ıes. That form of focused meditation
ıncrease your own abilities and can
comfort of your own home, without all of the
bells and whistles sometimes attributed to meditative trance.
Meditation is a wonderful instrument for accessing your
claircognizant gifts.

Exercise: Keep Your Head Together

Opening your crown chakra is painless, but it definitely requires some preparation. You don't want
to jump into this without first protecting yourself. When this seventh chakra opens, it becomes a
channel for spirit, and you want to be sure to pre-
vent negative entities or energy from easily stepping
through.

You'll need at least half an hour for this exercise,
so go somewhere you won't be disturbed and where
you can be comfortable. Bring your journal with
you. Then, sit or lie down and relax.

Begin by breathing. Take a nice deep breath and
imagine filling your lungs up with pure oxygen.
Know the oxygen that's flowing in is pushing out any
impurities and clearing your body of any debris that
doesn't belong there. As you exhale, focus on all of
the debris leaving your body, pushed out with your
breath through your mouth and all of your pores.
Continue breathing, steadily inhaling and exhaling,

all the while feeling the energy of the pure oxygen flowing into your lungs. Stay in this rhythm for at least five minutes, consciously focusing on your breath.

Now, bring all of your attention to the top of your head. Imagine you can feel the hair follicles pulsing with every breath. Feel the roots of your hair as they slowly begin to gently move and sway. Allow the sensation of the movement to flow down through the rest of your body, beginning with your third-eye chakra. Feel the warmth as it spreads around your forehead area. As your head becomes more tingly and your hair starts feeling like it's sticking straight up, let the energy move even farther down into your communication chakra, your throat area. Imagine seeing and feeling your throat opening, allowing clear passage for positive energy.

Next, bring the energy into your chest center, your healing chakra. Feel your heart expanding with every breath, breathing in and sending out healing throughout your body. Move that energy down into your solar plexus and allow any excess weight or debris to melt away as you feel the tingling spreading around your abdomen. Gently guide that positivity to your naval area and allow it to flow into your entire reproductive section. Then, move it all the way down to your base, or root chakra, between your legs at the bottom of your spine and allow the positive energy to flow up and reconnect, as if part of a circuit, to the top of your head, your crown.

As the stream of positive, healing, relaxing energy forms a complete circle, direct it to spread into a bubble all around your body. Envision it spreading out and encompassing your feet, your arms, and all the way up to the top of your head. This sphere of protection is now turning into a shimmery silver color, filled with pops of glittery sparkles of positive energy.

Now, imagine that the top of your head is loaded with hundreds of fiber-optic wires, puffing out of your crown, lit up with all different colors. Imagine these wires stretching out all around you, still protected by the silver, sparkly sphere, reaching toward the sky and the earth and everything in between. As they extend, feel the energy they draw in to your crown chakra, your claircognizant center.

What comes next is important. Believe that the answers you seek will be sent to you through the fiber-optic cables, just as your television receives a signal and broadcasts shows. Think of a question you want an answer to. It can be a request for which direction to go, when money will come in, what the best route to take will be for you professionally, whether you should have more children, etc. The wisdom you are looking for should be about you and should be personal. The answers you get will be incredible.

Did it feel right? Do you know what the outcome will be? Did you get the answer you expected? Are you excited? Sad? Happy? Disappointed? Try it again. Do it many times. Are you allowing yourself the space to just "know" the answer or are you trying to justify it? Enjoy the process. Don't question it. Let yourself go and you *will* just know.

Just Drive

Claircognizance, though highly difficult to always detect, is a gift well worth cultivating. Once recognized as a psychic sense, claircognizance can bring an unshakable wisdom or knowledge about many different areas in life. This clear knowing can tell you about a person you've just met, or the best look in your new kitchen, or when it's time to perform a maintenance check on your car.

Ellen, my client, experienced how this claircognizant sense worked firsthand after our session together. I was tuning in to her energy and getting a variety of information for her. But one thing stood out.

"I'm not sure what this means, but I know there's something going on with your car. Does this make sense to you? I'm getting that you need to do some type of maintenance," I suggested to Ellen.

"Hmmm. I'm not sure what that means," she replied.

"Okay. I know it's about maintenance. You need to do an oil change and something else. You need to check your tires. There's something going on with your tires; I think maybe you need to rotate them. Not sure exactly what will happen but I wouldn't put either of them off," I told her.

"All right. I will check it out."

About a week later I received an e-mail from Ellen. It said:

You mentioned that I should take care of my car. Nothing alarming, but do what needed to be done. I had "oil change & rotate tires" on my To Do list for months, so I decided I should take care of these things as you suggested. I took care of the oil change and when I went to Town Fair Tire to have my tires rotated (two different locations), they both said there was a two-hour wait and "come back Saturday at eight and we'll have you out in twenty minutes." Both places said that. So Saturday rolls around and it's raining and I decide to sleep in. That afternoon, I got a flat tire. I race to Town Fair on the spare and they are in the process of closing but say "if you come back at eight on Monday, we can have you out in twenty minutes." So I ended up there at eight on Monday AFTER ALL and got the flat repaired and my tires rotated. Can't help but think "someone" was pranking me! Plus, I was not expecting a charge for a flat repair and had very little cash on me. The charge came to $4.20. I had three $1 bills on me and EXACTLY $1.20 in change—I was down to counting pennies but had the right amount. I don't know what all this means but I was laughing—I definitely felt like something was going on!!!

I couldn't explain to Ellen how I knew she was going to have problems except to share how claircognizance works. Sometimes this clear knowing produces precognitive flashes of insight. Precognition is being able to discern events in the future that have not yet occurred and of which you have no previous knowledge. The precognitive knowing I had for Ellen helped her, though putting off the tire rotation may have unintentionally caused the flat that I had alluded to in her reading.

Exercise: What Do You Know?

It is your chance to read your own future. If you've been looking externally, to other people, in order to determine an event or a decision, it's time for a change. Now, you can do it for yourself.

As always, go somewhere comfortable and begin by breathing deeply. Focus on the top of your head. Imagine there is a huge silver funnel of energy emerging from your crown chakra and spreading out to the universe. Place a circle of white light all around you, surrounding you and protecting you from any negativity. When you're sure you are fully shielded, take another deep breath and continue.

For this exercise you need to trust the answers you are getting are real and they are coming to you claircognizantly. You will experience the answers through clear knowing, rather than hearing or seeing them.

Think of a question regarding your future—a situation, a person, etc. Ask the question, and while you do, believe that you will receive the response. It may take a moment or two, but you will be blessed with a clear sense of knowing the answer.

Once you're confident you know the answer to your question, ask another one. Wait until you are positive you absolutely know the response. Keep going until you no longer know the answers or you get tired. Don't ask more than five questions during one sitting. The answers tend to get convoluted, and it's tricky to ascertain if you are using your claircognizance or a different psychic sense.

If you've received your answers in a way other than clear knowing, that's all right. That can happen if you have one or two other strong senses. They key is to persevere. Don't give up if it doesn't work right away. You can take the entire week to really focus in on your sense of knowing.

If you did attain your answers through your claircognizance, more power to you! This is great. Again, give yourself the week to work on your clear knowing. This may prove to be your most utilized psychic ability in your intuitive tool kit.

A Boutique?

All of the psychic senses can contribute to precognizant flashes, but clear knowing is sometimes more difficult to identify. Becoming acquainted with the sensation you experience when you know something is key to discovering this intuitive gift. When you are having a true claircognizant moment, it will come from outside; you are merely observing the information rather than actually generating the thoughts. Claircognizant knowing can defy logic; there may be absolutely no reason you can fathom that you are receiving the information. It may have no connection whatsoever to anything you are thinking or that you're involved with at the current time.

After I graduated high school, I worked full time in accounting and went to college at night and on the weekends. I was all set to be an accountant, a profession I subsequently worked in for eleven years. I prepared taxes for a public accounting firm and then went on to be the controller of a company. Before I began my career as an accountant, I was in my senior year of high school and all of a sudden I had a knowing that I would own a boutique. Anyone who knew me at the time knew that although I enjoyed the latest fashions and usually dressed to impress when I went out I really wasn't planning on owning my own store, and certainly not one that may have required me to go into the city to purchase clothing. I doubted the claircognizant impression I had. There was no way I would work in or own a boutique of any kind.

Years later, while I was working, I had another clear knowing. I would own the store and it would be colorful. Again, this came out of the blue, and I doubted its validity. I decided it was just my imagination or possibly it was connected to someone else. I ignored it.

I got married and three months later became pregnant with my first baby. From the moment I became pregnant, I started thinking about quitting my job. I knew, without reservation, there was no way I wanted to remain where I was after my baby was born. But I had no idea what I would do. I knew I still needed to work, as we needed two incomes. We had purchased a new home right before we were married and the mortgage was not going to pay itself. I also knew there was no way I wanted to leave my soon-to-be daughter all day long. Still, I had no plan until one day immediately after my first baby was born.

I was visiting my sister, about a half hour from where I lived, and we went to a children's consignment store.

Instantly after walking through the door, I knew exactly what I was going to do. I was going to open a children's consignment store. I quickly did research and began acquiring inventory. I located a space and my husband and I outfitted it. I quit my job and had my grand opening. Then I realized, this was my boutique. My bright, multicolored painted floor and rainbow-hued walls confirmed it.

I hadn't believed it possible when I initially had the claircognizant impressions, but I should have. Sometimes it's all about timing. If I'd had the precognizant flash and began looking for something else it would've altered my life and I may never have worked as an accountant, married my husband, had my baby, opened the children's consignment store, or even had my next baby. It would all have been different. Looking back, I recognize those clear knowing moments as incredible claircognizant gifts. Looking forward, I hope to remain open to more.

Journaling can help us recognize these seventh chakra hits. By writing these spur-of-the-moment, out-of-the-blue perceptions down it becomes easier to distinguish when they happen. Creating the space to open your claircognitive and precognitive flashes furthers their occurrence and more importantly allows them to become more ordinary or second nature.

Exercise: Write What You Know

Think back to a time when you knew something but doubted it. It can be as significant as my story with the boutique or it can be something as simple as knowing you'd play a sport when you had no natural

inclination or desire toward it then you found y
self participating later in life. Though you are mainly
using your claircognizance, you may find other psychic senses creep in as well, especially if your knowing included a vision. That's okay. The main point to
this exercise is to begin writing it all down and recognizing that these claircognizant flashes may also
be precognitive knowings.

Try remembering the time frame involved. Did it
take years to have your precognition come to fruition,
as was the case in my story? Or did it happen quickly?
Or has it even come to pass? If it has happened, what
changes might it have made in your life if you'd acted
on it sooner rather than later? Or even later instead of
sooner? Did it make your life easier? Better? Worse?
Did it affect someone else?

Write down everything you can think of that is
relevant. Then, do it again. Is there another time you
had a claircognizant or precognizant impression?
Record it now.

Automatic Writing

Once you become accustomed to journaling and the writing starts to flow more effortlessly, you may find yourself
writing words that you weren't intending or sentences that
do not seemingly originate from your own thoughts. You
may have stumbled upon automatic writing. Automatic
writing is another way to access your claircognizance and
is a great way to receive answers to any questions you may
have.

Automatic writing is a way to channel your higher self. It's also an accessible way to receive assistance from your spirit guides, angels, deceased loved ones from the other side, and the universe. This type of freestyle writing gives you the opportunity and format to tune in to your clear knowing in a manner that is noninvasive and nonthreatening. Automatic writing provides you with the means to tune in to your soul. That's a pretty incredible ability.

An easy way to use automatic writing, also known as channeled, soul, or spirit writing, is to start by asking a question. This form of communicating with your spirit can be a little confusing in the beginning. It may feel, again, as so often claircognizance can, that it's just your imagination. You might continue to feel as if you are just making it up. Eventually, you will find yourself receiving messages you had no way to know. This is true automatic writing.

Intent is what sets channeled writing apart from regular journaling. As you journal, you are writing about what you're already aware of or are already thinking about. With soul writing, you are tapping into the wisdom of the universe in order to satisfy or access your claircognizance. In addition—and sometimes more importantly—it is a purposeful or purpose-driven practice to uncover your deepest-seated knowledge, the wisdom you've carried with you throughout all of your lifetimes. Occasionally, the queries you write will provide you with replies you never expected. Channeled writing can also give you directions on how to achieve whatever you've asked about.

The more you practice the art of spirit writing, the more proficient you will be. What begins as pages of conscious journaling before receiving possibly only one or two mystical answers can turn into one or two conscious words immediately followed by soul wisdom.

"Sometimes you will even receive answers to questions you were only thinking of asking. This phenomenon is well documented among other divinatory processes, commonly called 'Psychic Override,' and is your Higher Self's way of communicating an important message to you that it might not otherwise have the chance to do," says Edain McCoy. (McCoy, 1994)

The only way to experience automatic writing and to truly understand it is to do it. Like many things paranormal or psychic, practicing it brings knowledge and, more significantly, it brings excitement, enjoyment, and fun.

Exercise: Practicing Automatic Writing

Get out a new journal or multiple pieces of paper. Then, bring your circle of protection around you as you breathe in and out. Now, in your relaxed state take another breath. Put your pen to paper and write the following words:

"Dear Universe,
I'd really love to connect to the infinite wisdom that resides within me and around me. I am excited to share in whatever knowledge you wish to channel through me. I am sincerely thankful and filled with gratitude and appreciation for everything I have and everything to come. I am ready and open and eager for any messages you have for me."

Now, let the words flow. Begin writing whatever comes to mind, whatever flows from your pen. Even if it feels like you are consciously writing, continue. Don't stop. It's okay. It may take a page or two before you are no longer concentrating on what you're writing. The words will just begin to flow and spirit will be directing your pen.

If you find after writing a couple of pages (or for at least ten minutes) that you are still consciously processing everything, stop. Take a breath. Put your pen down.

Next, think of a question you'd like an answer to. Try not to make it something you already know the answer to. If you were to receive a different response than you know to be true, it will turn you off. Go through the same process. Begin by writing down your question. Then try and take your mind out of it and let your hand begin to move. Again, if it feels like your imagination it's all right. Just keep going. Give yourself at least ten minutes.

Use this exercise a few times this week to really make it work for you and to make the connection. Once you do, you will know. When you read it back, you may not even recognize the style of writing as it won't necessarily be your own.

On the Edge

About two decades ago, before all of this started for me, I experienced a shift. This shift left me feeling a bit empty, although I knew there was some kind of energy revving up within me and around me. I couldn't quite grasp what was missing or what was happening, but I knew there was something huge going on. I felt as though I was on the edge of something, about to jump into a whole new world. It seemed as though that edge was moving, keeping just enough distance from me that I couldn't quite move past it but close enough that I felt its tantalizing pull on my psyche.

This thing, this elusive edge, was taunting me—drawing me toward what I knew promised to be something incredible, yet at the same time keeping itself protected. This cliff I was dying to dive off of was elusive, but I was able to catch glimmers of knowing it was there, every day, multiple times a day. It got to the point that it felt as though I could taste it, just like when you have a word on the tip of your tongue but you can't quite vocalize it. I was unable to translate in feelings or words what the edge was or, more importantly, what was on the other side of this cliff. This, understandably, was making me crazy. I wanted to understand. I craved clarity. I needed to know.

Then, just like that, it became fully and inexorably apparent exactly what I was on the edge of. I knew, without a doubt, what was on the other side of the cliff and what would be there when I dove in. The universe was waiting for me. In its infinite wisdom, it was ready to show me the secrets of the world, one small step at a time. I was ready to tune in to the energy. I knew that I knew, though I didn't quite know yet what that meant.

It was shortly after that when I felt as if I was hit over the head and told, "You need to do this work now." That was the beginning of something great, something incredible. I dove in, without regard to what the future held, because I trusted it would be fantastic and totally worth putting my energy into. That was the first time I really understood what claircognizance felt like: that clear knowing, the total comprehension and understanding of something you really have no business knowing or any prior knowledge of. I just knew my life was inescapably altered from that moment on. And if I were to trust that, it would be so much better.

After that initial knowing, that deep subconscious coming to terms with the inevitable, I began experiencing more of those knowing moments at the edge of something incredible. I started having moments of perfect clarity that left me knowing there was more change coming, though I couldn't quite put my finger on the next step. I realized, though it wasn't and still isn't complete, that each cliff, or each edge brings me to a new aspect of my extrasensory life. These periods, which can be fleeting moments of knowing or may take months or even years to come to fruition and understand, bring with them a keen sense of desire, of wanting to know whatever it is I am supposed to know. And I find myself receiving bread crumbs of knowledge that are eventually and naturally strung together to form the claircognizant beliefs, bringing me to my next level of psychic ability or introducing me to the next step in my path of my spiritual journey.

This knowing that there's more to the life we're living brings with it a sense of expectancy that can be so strong it's almost painful. The yearning to know, without a shadow of a doubt, what's on the other side of the cliff is almost overpowering. Knowing without rhyme or reason that something's coming is very powerful. It helps to propel you to the next level or the next achievement. It gives you the desire and even the wherewithal to continue plugging forward, regardless of the obstacles, to make something incredible happen. This knowing makes you believe that there's more to life than the everyday doldrums you may have been experiencing or even the happy daily routine you've found yourself participating in. You know there's more to it. You know you are getting ready for an awakening.

That's what it is. I'm sure of it. It is an awakening of spirit—a charging of our spiritual batteries that is like a trickle charger rather than an ER crash cart. It's a methodical handing out of knowledge from the universe, allowing us time to grasp each step before we move on to the next level. We are, each and every one of us, awakening to the greatness we have inside us, hooking us into the infinite wisdom that's within us and around us throughout the vast universe. We are all beginning, at our own pace, to know.

Exercise: On the Edge

Have you ever felt like you were on the edge of something? That there was something coming and you just knew it? That, even though you weren't totally sure what it was you knew, it would be something good or even great? When was the last time this happened to you? Remember, knowing doesn't always mean you know what it specifically is that you're on the edge of, but it does mean you know something is revving up, that there's an energy getting ready to blow up, in a good way.

Write down the last time this happened, this knowing that you were about to enter a new phase of life or that something was about to open up for you. What was the new phase? How did it feel leading up to it? Did you have an idea what it would be? How did you feel after it happened? Did it make you happy? Or did it make you not feel good? Was it worth the buildup? How did you know it was happening? Write down anything else you can remember about feeling like you were on the edge of change.

Was there another time in your life you felt that way? Another awakening moment? If so, record that as well!

Are You on the Edge?

My client Jordan is experiencing being on the edge. She's been coming to me for a few months, and we've been working on many different aspects of her spirituality. She is not a beginner, not by any means. She is a Reiki Master and tunes in to energy through the use of her Tibetan bowls. Jordan knows she is on a path. We've been exploring her psychic abilities and she's discovering truths about herself that she can now work on. She's striving to be the best she can be by utilizing her psychic senses.

Jordan knows she is on the verge of entering a new phase in her life. Right now, she can feel it. She knows, as she also describes it, that she's on the edge of something; that greatness is almost within her grasp. She just doesn't know exactly what that greatness is or what she will become when she dives into the other side. But she is ready. Jordan wants this so bad she can taste it. What I find even more incredible is she expresses her feelings to me—her knowing—in exactly the same way I explained my own sense of knowing I was on that cliff, yet she wasn't aware of my own awakening.

Having the knowing, that belief that you are on the edge of another phase in your life, can bring excitement to your everyday world. Getting ready to dive into the newest aspect of your being may bring a bit of anxiety as well. This state of being feels as though you're constantly waiting: waiting for the other shoe to drop, waiting for something extraordinary to happen, or even just waiting, afraid to miss whatever it is that is coming. This alone can make you feel jittery. But knowing there's more to life, more to come, makes all of the nerves worth it.

When you have this claircognizant sense of knowing, there's no holding back the need to search for whatever it is you feel is coming. You can find yourself looking, even investigating different avenues that might seem to be leading you to what you need. This is good. Often, it is during the hunt for what's on the other side of the cliff that you learn more about yourself and your psychic senses. This seemingly ever-elusive claircognizant vibe that can make you a little crazy should also be used to help you access your psychic sense. You can learn to access it.

Exercise: What's Waiting for You?

Similar to the last exercise, this time you are going to focus on that knowing feeling of being on the edge by creating that edge. As always, breathe deeply to put yourself into a relaxed state. Then circle yourself with white light to protect yourself from any negativity.

Now, imagine in your mind an actual cliff. Then, focus in on that cliff and what it looks like, feels like, and smells like. Next, imagine on the other side is the answer to unlocking a new phase in your life. Believe that you can know what that new phase is. Once you begin getting a feeling for what is on the other side, tune in to it. It's time to know what you need to do next.

After you know what's waiting for you when you pass the initial border, it's time to see beyond the next perimeter. You may practice this exercise a few times, but don't do it too often. You need to give yourself time to bring your knowing to fruition rather than trying to rush it and not fulfilling your next step. Above all, enjoy the anticipation that's present. Give yourself enough time to feel that sense of knowing before you move on.

All Knowing

Claircognizance generally is one of the most difficult psychic senses to recognize. Mostly this is because you are not seeing or hearing anything. Rather, you just need to trust what you know to be without understanding why you know it or having any reason behind what it is that you know. However, claircognizance is also one of the most definitive psychic senses because when it hits, you just know whatever it is you are meant to know without having to figure it out.

six

Clairgustance (Clear Tasting)

"Taste life, it's delicious."

—UNKNOWN

Have you ever tasted something even though there was nothing in your mouth? Sounds strange, right? Well, it is. But clairgustance, in its basic form, refers to tasting something that's not actually in your mouth. This is an unusual psychic sense, but it can also be a helpful one. Unlike the more prominent psychic senses, clairgustance may seem bizarre.

Seldom does clairgustance work by itself. It rarely presents itself alone, without the accompaniment of another intuitive sense. This remarkable gift often serves to enhance our other psychic senses. For example, a taste may evoke a clairvoyant vision (see chapter 2) or a clairsentient feeling (see chapter 4). Commonly, clairgustance is experienced in tandem with clairalience, or clear smelling (see chapter 7). Our physical sense of smell enhances our physical sense of taste, so it follows suit that the same would hold true in the extrasensory realm.

I was given evidence of just this fact during a phone session I was doing recently with a lovely young woman named Bambi. We'd been talking for about half an hour, and she was able to validate everything I told her. Mostly I was discussing things I'd seen clairvoyantly, felt clairsentiently, known claircognizantly, or heard clairaudiently. The next thing I psychically received was different—I was tasting something.

"I'm tasting citrus—more specifically oranges. What does this mean to you?" I asked Bambi.

"I'm not eating oranges. I mean, I like them, but I can't imagine what it could be," she answered.

"Okay, well, now I'm also tasting what seems to be Thanksgiving dinner," I continued, knowing there had to be a reason for it.

"I don't know. We don't usually have oranges during Thanksgiving dinner. I'm not sure what that is," Bambi said. "Maybe you're just hungry?"

We chuckled at that. After all, admittedly I was hungry. But I knew there was more to it than something that simple. So, I tuned in to my other senses to fill in the blanks. What I saw was the shape of Florida. I felt myself being pulled from Florida to Connecticut.

"Is someone visiting from Florida?" I asked her. "I feel like your father is trying to let you know he'll be there for this. I believe it will be before Thanksgiving but in November," I said. Now I was sure of the orange and Thanksgiving tastes I had.

"Oh, yes! Of course. I don't know why I didn't get it! My sister is coming up from Florida before Thanksgiving. It should be a great visit!" Bambi shared, comforted by the validation that her father was still around and able to be with them in spirit.

The clairgustatory impressions I received led me to the location of Florida as well as the November time frame. The phantom tastes introduced me to my next psychic hit. Clairgustance was the primary means to let me share with Bambi what her father wanted her to know: that he would be around them for their family gathering.

Exercise: Sweet or Sour?

Foods have different flavors. Those flavors can be categorized as citrusy, sweet, spicy, savory, sour, etc. One at a time, think of each food collection. Imagine you are eating something that matches that food group. For example, citrus can be oranges or lemons, sweet can be chocolate, and spicy can be a chili pepper. Make your own connection and make it strong. Allow your taste buds to salivate and really believe you are chewing on the food you've allocated to each flavor.

Do it again using different foods. Do some tastes come across stronger than others? Are some more prominent? Are some of the flavor groups more difficult to taste? Practicing will help you recognize the different flavors when you actually experience clairgustance.

Cinnamon Spaghetti

One of the most common reasons mediums experience clairgustance is to recognize someone through taste. Imagine trying to determine who you are tuning in to during a séance and you taste chicken noodle soup. This can be translated by thinking symbolically, as in whoever is trying to come through was a "chicken," but chances are it instead represents Grandma who was known for her chicken noodle soup or whom you've regularly shared this soup with.

I was doing a reading for an older gentleman named Tim. He had been in my office for about forty-five minutes and I hadn't connected to anyone from the other side, per se. It was all about his past, present, and future life. He asked me if there was anything else.

"All of a sudden I am tasting something kind of strange. I want to say I am eating pasta with a normal meat sauce, but there's more to it," I told him.

"I don't know what that means. I haven't had pasta for quite a while. I'm not having any gluten anymore, so I rarely have macaroni," he responded. "Unless there's more to it. Is it because it's brown rice or gluten-free pasta? My daughter has been making me crazy lately—everything's all about staying away from anything with white flour," he said with a smile.

"Hmmm. I don't think that's what it is. Maybe my taste buds are off, but I feel like there's an unusual ingredient in the pasta or the sauce," I continued. "Does this make sense to you?"

"I'm not really sure. I can't imagine what it could be," he said, a bit disappointed that I hadn't connected to anyone.

"I know this sounds crazy, but I taste nutmeg and cinnamon in the spaghetti sauce," I said, feeling there was no way this would ring true, at all.

"Oh my goodness! I know exactly what that is!" Tim responded, and I watched a tear roll down his cheek.

"Wow, I'm glad because I've never tasted anything like this before," I told him, feeling confused but happy because it obviously meant something important to him.

"You've just connected to my late wife," he whispered.

"Really? Was that a normal recipe? It seems strange," I countered.

"On one of our first dates ever she told me she wanted to cook for me. I had asked her if she was any good and she answered that she really wasn't but she wanted to try anyway. She told me I was worth the effort," he shared, more tears moistening his eyes as well as his face.

"So were the nutmeg and cinnamon part of the dessert?" I asked.

"No," he laughed. "She had never made homemade pasta sauce so she didn't want to go that far. But she didn't want to serve me just jarred sauce, so she decided she would doctor it up with some spices. She had no idea which ones to use, so she grabbed the ones near the front. Those were nutmeg and cinnamon. When I got to her apartment she had the table set beautifully, candles and all. We sat down and took the first bite and both of us practically spit it out! We were definitely not expecting what we experienced in our mouths! It was an explosion of flavor, but not in a good way! Well, we both cracked up, ate dinner anyway, and the rest is history. We laughed about that quite a bit before she died."

"What a wonderful story! I definitely think this is her way of coming through to let you know she's around. She's also letting us know that she still has her sense of humor!"

"Oh, yes. She had a wonderful sense of humor. I miss that the most, I think," he told me with a smile.

His connection was made. The love of his life had come through with a private message that only he could have known. This was total validation that his wife was around, continuing their shared experiences and recognizing a pivotal, life-changing time for both of them. Might she have come through in a different way? Of course. But she chose to share something special and made me taste her presence, which became the best part of the reading.

Having a deceased loved one come through is great. Clairgustance can also act as a precognitive tool. Along the same lines as tasting the strange pasta sauce, imagine tasting your best friend's favorite food, having that phantom flavor in your mouth. You haven't seen or heard from this best friend in a year because you've both been so busy and you've moved away from each other. But now you have this taste in your mouth of your best friend's food, and it's been there all day. Next thing you know, you open up your computer and there's an e-mail from just that person telling you they are coming to visit next week! That's precognitive clairgustance.

Tasting something that's not actually in your mouth is one of the prevalent forms of clairgustance. Interpreting what you taste is important. Recognizing that flavor and matching it to a person, a time frame, or a life event is vital to understanding the meaning behind the taste. Learning how to translate it is fundamentally key.

Exercise: Trying Out Clairgustance

Get out a pen and your journal. Open up to a fresh page. On the top of the page write "Clairgustance." Now, think of ten people. They can be dead or alive, family or friends. Write down their names, leaving plenty of room to write under each one.

Then, connect tastes with everyone on your list, one by one. If you wrote down your husband's name and his favorite food is mint chocolate chip ice cream, write that down. The point to this exercise is to associate each person with a specific taste that you can recognize. Keep going until you've finished all ten people. If you've written down additional names, complete those as well.

When you're all done, go back over your list. Do the tastes you've specified truly fit with the person you've connected them to? If you're sure, then move on to the next step. If you need to make some changes, now's your chance to do it.

Next, go back over each person on your list. Can you taste the food in your mouth? Does it make sense to you? Does it taste like the real thing? If you're having a difficult time tasting the various foods, take it to the next level and actually make or buy the food and eat it so you can specifically recognize the taste. As you are experiencing the flavors, whether physically or psychically, think of the person you've connected to it. Be sure to really lock in the flavor with the person. From now on, using your clairgustance, you will easily be able to link each person with their food.

Changing Taste

Have you ever tasted something that didn't taste the way it normally should? Or had something to eat that made you think of someone or something? This is another form of clairgustance: to actually eat something and have it trigger something else. Now, I'm not talking about how my sister's potato salad makes me think of my grandmother because she's the only one in the family who can even come close to reproducing the flavor and texture. I'm speaking, rather, of the flavor composition tasting entirely different than it ought to.

Sometimes the flavors can even change while you're eating, from minute to minute. You may start off eating a cheeseburger and having it actually taste like a cheeseburger. But then, it tastes like you are eating black raspberry ice cream. And then, after a few bites, it starts to resemble squash or zucchini. This can be unusual, but not unheard of.

I've attended many different classes at the Omega Institute for Holistic Studies. While there, students sleep in dormitory-style rooms or mostly shared semiprivate rooms. The workshops can last anywhere from a weekend to an entire week. Included in the cost are tuition, room, and board; the dining hall serves breakfast, lunch, and dinner. Inside and on the extremely large porch are many round tables that people occupy. Everyone sits with a variety of students from all of the classes whom they may or may not know. It was during one of these stays that I had a clairgustatory experience.

I was sitting at a table with about seven other people whom I didn't recognize or know. They were not part of my class for the week. Some were in a cooking class and some were in yoga. But they were all interested in what I was doing there. So, I told them. I was there for a psychic workshop and we were talking to dead people. Now, some people are skeptical, myself included, so they wanted proof. I told them, just as I tell everyone, "You're welcome to believe or not believe. It's entirely up to you."

"So, is there anyone with us now?" one of them asked.

"Ha ha. I'm not tuning in right now. I'm just trying to eat my lunch!" I laughed.

"All right. It's not something that happens automatically? I thought you could just pick something up out of the blue," another shared honestly.

"Sometimes, but usually I focus in on the connection to make it strong," I continued, explaining that if I was "on" all of the time I would never be able to live in the present moment.

As we sat there eating our salads, I remarked on how delicious it was. As everyone was busy mhmm-ing and agreeing, I realized the salad didn't taste the same. The lettuces and the other vegetables that had moments ago tasted fresh now tasted moldy, almost musty. Then, I began tasting strawberries, which expanded into strawberry shortcake.

"That's strange. I just got a really musty taste and now I taste strawberry shortcake," I explained to the group at the table. "Does anyone else's salad taste strange?"

Everyone shook their head no. Their salads were still delicious.

"Wait. Did you say musty and strawberry shortcake?" one of the people at the table asked.

"Yes, why? Does your food taste like that, too?"

"No, but my mother always talked about how her food always tasted moldy and musty. Nothing tasted good; everything was very unappetizing. The only food that tasted relatively normal and was appetizing was strawberry shortcake. So, we prepared that for her at least twice a week and made sure she always had fresh strawberries on hand," she replied, amazed.

"Wow. I taste something that I can only describe as sick or ill in my mouth. It tastes like what I would imagine cancer would taste like. But I'm also feeling a lot of love."

"That's what made her taste buds bad and what she eventually died from. She had cancer. Oh my God. I can't believe she came through that way," she explained with tears in her eyes. "Thank you for that. I know she is trying to tell me she is here and that's so what I needed to hear!"

This was one of the first times I ever experienced clairgustance in this way. My food literally started tasting different. It wasn't just a phantom taste; my salad actually changed its flavor. With every bite I took, I tasted something unusual. This episode of clairgustance helped bring comfort to someone who was really looking for validation that there was more to life than what we live here on Earth. I was able to prove to her, without even trying, that her mother was still around and that her spirit was present with her and that she was sharing her love.

Exercise: Sensing Tastes

This will be a culinary experiment. One that will get your clairgustatory juices flowing. Get together with a friend for lunch or dinner. You are going to be eating a meal, but this time, with a twist. Have your friend write down at least twenty different foods on separate slips of paper and fold them up so you can't see them.

During your meal, something you really enjoy, pick a piece of paper and look at what food is written down. Now, focus in on that flavor as you continue to eat your meal. Can you taste the new flavor? Are you able to almost negate the flavor of what you're eating to taste the flavor listed on the paper? Tell your friend what's recorded and see if they also can taste the new flavor. Try this with all of the foods your partner has listed, but be sure to eat your meal and actually taste it between each other food.

Do you find some of the foods are easier to experience than others? Does it seem like the saltier ones come through better or the sweet? Did your friend find it to be the same? Or did they have a harder time with the ones that seemed to be easier for you?

As a bonus, did any of the flavors evoke feelings of someone you know or someone who's passed? Did they remind you of an event or a time in your life? Remember, by learning to recognize and tune in to the flavors you are developing your clairgustance!

What Flavor Is Your Name?

All of the situations above are forms of clairgustance. The phantom tastes and the morphing of flavors are probably the most common of clairgustatory evidence. Experiencing clairgustance to determine something more specific is also possible and happened during one of my sessions many, many years ago.

My client John came in. He was hoping to connect to his mother, who had passed. I was able to tune in to others in his life, both living and dead. By using a combination of my other psychic senses, I provided him with initials and actual names, but I just wasn't getting anything about his mom. So we moved on to discussing his future regarding his career.

"Is there a reason I'd be tasting peppermint?" I asked John.

"Not that I know of," he responded.

"Are you looking for a job where they make mints? Or medicine? Or even peppermint mouthwash?" I continued.

"Maybe. I guess it's a possibility. I don't really know where I'm going to apply yet, but I'll keep peppermint in mind," John answered.

I told him that would be a good idea, and then we moved on again to where he would be moving. The first items I had picked up on during his psychic reading were that he wanted to change jobs and move out of state.

"I'm feeling more up north, toward Canada, like Vermont or upper New York State. Does this make sense?" I queried.

"Actually, yes! I have been considering moving that way because I love the winter weather and would be very happy to be able to ski right out of my door!" he replied, excited to hear that what he was hoping to do sounded like a definite possibility.

"Great! Maybe that's what the peppermint is? I'm still getting it. Maybe candy canes or hot chocolate with peppermint? I can't help it. This peppermint taste keeps coming through!" I told him. "Now, maybe it's just because I have bad breath from all of this talking and the spirits are trying to brighten it up so I don't disgust you, but I feel like there's more to it!" I laughed, still trying to figure it all out.

"Ha! Your breath is just fine!" he chuckled.

"Okay, one more try; is your sugar level low? Are you hypoglycemic? I'm not only tasting the peppermint, but I'm hearing Peppermint Patty."

"No, my sugars are generally very normal," John said.

"Hmm. I think I finally get it. This taste has not gone away. The peppermint flavor is there. It's not going away. Was your mom's name Patty?" I asked.

"Oh my gosh! Leave it to her to be so tricky! She was always a joker. This makes perfect sense now. Her name was Patricia but everyone called her Patty. Wow. Thanks for showing up, Mom!"

Patty made sure we validated her presence before she let me stop tasting peppermint. I didn't understand it right away, but she kept the flavor there. I was able to use my clairgustance after all of my other psychic senses had failed to produce the name of John's mother. I have to admit, I'm glad she wasn't referring to *A Fish Called Wanda* or something. Tasting fish all through the reading would have been gross!

Exercise: Write Down the Flavor

Take out your journal and begin recording any food, candy, book, movie, etc., that has food and name reference. You can start off by using candies such as "Peppermint Patty" and "Mary Jane" and take it from there. You may want to include "Oscar Mayer Wiener." List every one you can think of and then ask your family and friends for any others they can think of that you may have missed. Now that you know how many connections there are between brands of foods or movies or books with names you may find that you link with someone you know who may be alive or dead.

When you're all done, practice tasting the flavors based on the names you've written down. For example, can you taste peppermint when you think of Peppermint Patty? Begin associating the flavors with different names and/or people and record those in your journal as well.

Clairgustance for Your Mind, Body, and Spirit

Your psychic ability to tune in through taste is not limited to connecting for other people or communicating with the other side. This clairgustatory sense can also be used to tap into your mind, body, and spirit to determine what you need to add or even what you need to take away.

Whether you connect to your clairgustance for health reasons or other purposes, you should know that your fifth chakra or throat chakra not only connects to your clairaudience (see chapter 3), it's also connected to your clairgustance. Focusing in on this area, this communication chakra, will assist you with opening up your clairgustatory sense.

I am a hypnotist as well as a psychic. This means I work with people for a variety of reasons. I often have people who come in looking for hypnosis for weight loss. When we begin to explore their current eating habits and their exercise patterns, more often than not they've already been dieting and working out. This, usually, is not the problem. Frequently they are there because they have no idea what they need to do. This is where I connect my hypnotism skills with my intuition.

I tune in to their energy and try and determine what foods might better serve them and which they should avoid. I do this not only to help them limit their caloric intake, but also to ascertain which foods will allow them to feel healthier overall—mind, body, and spirit. The funny thing is, I find I'm not necessarily limiting them to fruit, vegetables, and protein; I regularly taste chocolate as well! Chocolate is, after all, a food group.

Exercise: Help Yourself

It's your turn to help yourself now. Go somewhere that you won't be disturbed and get comfortable. Bring your journal with you so you can record the relevant information to review later.

Focus on your throat chakra. Bring a brilliant blue color there and imagine it is spreading from your neck, glowing from the inside out. Allow this communication and taste center to open fully and to expand wide. Then, think about your overall health. You are going to ask the essential question, "What do I need for my body, mind, and spirit?"

After you ask this, say, "First, I would like to taste what my body needs to feel and be better on the whole." Then wait. Notice if you begin to experience any tastes or flavors in your mouth. If not, go back to imagining the blue light expanding from your throat chakra, and as it does thank the universe for giving you the opportunity to taste whatever you need to by focusing on your neck area.

Try it again. Ask what you need for your body. Once you taste something focus in on it until you are sure you know what the flavor is. Then move on to the next one. Ask what you need for your mind. Follow the same procedure for this one and give yourself time to truly tune in with your clairgustance. Finally, ask what you need for your spirit. Are any of the flavors the same? Are they all different? Did you get something for each of them? Do the flavors seem to make sense?

Are you able to relate the flavors to specific foods, herbs, or drinks? Or, are you barely able to grasp the taste? Write down whatever foods, spices, drinks, herbs, etc., your clairgustance provided you for your mind, body, and spirit. Do they feel right to you? Does it seem like these foods may help make you better in some way?

Clairgustance as a Vessel?

All of your psychic senses can transport you to a place distant in time and space. Clairgustance is no different in theory, but it is different in how it works. Have you ever had anything strange occur while eating? Occasionally, with clairgustance, you may feel like you are experiencing something that you aren't physically going through. This is a very rare type of clairgustance, but it does happen.

Imagine eating a hot dog and immediately feeling like you were no longer sitting at your dining room table but were in the middle of Yankee Stadium. Or even on the streets of New York, almost like you were transported there. That bite of the hot dog, that taste, brought you to another place. This, too, is clairgustance, and it has happened to me.

Remembering a time when you tasted the same flavor is different than having a true clairgustatory experience. You may eat pumpkin ice cream and remember the time you shared it with your mom twenty years ago. That's *not* clairgustance; that's nostalgia. However, if you eat pumpkin ice cream and feel like you are transported back to that time twenty years ago with your mom, that *is* absolutely clairgustance. It's almost like, for a brief time, you are in that time and place.

When I was young, we used to have a set lunch schedule in elementary school. I remember on Mondays we'd have pasta with meat sauce and Fridays were pizza days. That meat sauce had a very distinct flavor. I truly believe they snuck liver into the sauce, though no one ever admitted it. About ten years ago, I was away at a seminar and I ran out for a quick lunch at a roadside food stop. I had placed my order and brought it back to my car to eat. It wasn't pasta, it was a meatball grinder, but it had the same flavor. I remember thinking it tasted familiar. Then, all of a sudden, I felt like I was standing in the school cafeteria, looking around at all of the students. I could tell I was there as my adult self, back in a time when I was a child. Though it only lasted for a brief second, it felt very real. That was a very strange experience, but one I would welcome again.

This form of clairgustance is very rare. It involves astral travel—your spirit going to a place distant in time and space while your body stays where it is. Astral travel is more commonly brought on while in a more relaxed state such as sleep or meditation. I was in my car, eating my lunch.

Exercise: Where Do These Food Memories Take You?

The first step to experiencing this form of transportation clairgustance is to determine what flavors bring on which memories. Get your journal out and open it to a fresh page. Across the top, write "Memories of Food." Then, one by one, leaving plenty of room to fill in the necessary descriptions, write down foods that hold distinct memories.

For example, there is an event called the Oyster Festival in Connecticut that is held on the water every year. There are arts and crafts, shows, music, and more. But one reason people go is because of the extraordinary amount of food stands. There are two very distinct flavors that always make me reminiscent of the Oyster Festival. One is pizza fritas and the other is the baked potato, fully loaded with chili, broccoli, bacon, cheese, and sour cream. These two foods will always evoke memories of being at the Oyster Festival.

Write down the foods that give you these types of reminiscent feelings. After you've written them down go back and fill in the blanks. Where does it remind you of? How old were you? Were you with anyone? What were you doing? Was it a happy time? A sad time? Were you excited? Were you having fun? Does it remind you of being somewhere with someone who has since died? Write down everything you can remember about that specific food and then move on to the next one. You may find yourself adding more to the list. This is great! Continue remembering as long as you want.

Taste This

You are now a clairgustatory connoisseur. You've taken a fundamental necessity like food and utilized it as an even more natural intuitive gift. Though clairgustance may be a

154 · Chapter Six

rarer or more unique form of psychic sense, it can easily bring through quite a bit of desired or even much-needed information.

Clear taste can be useful to mediums because it can assist in bringing through deceased loved ones from the other side. It can be helpful to the medical profession by assisting them with a diagnosis or a direction to look to determine what's wrong with a patient, as I mentioned in the introduction. It can even be helpful to law enforcement; imagine working a murder case and tasting the last food the victim, or more importantly, the murderer, ate, bringing them that much closer to the time right before death. It can evoke memories and even transport you to another time or place in your life that can make you happy. Clairgustance can even alert you precognitively of an upcoming visit or something even more important. Paying attention to your clairgustance will always be beneficial and may even make you look at food in a whole new way. You should taste everything life has to offer.

seven

Clairalience/Clairolfaction/ Clairescence (Clear Smelling)

*"That which we call a rose
by any other name would smell as sweet."*
—WILLIAM SHAKESPEARE

Clairalience, also known as clairolfaction and clairescence, means clear smell. Just as we have our physical sense of smell, we also have a corresponding psychic sense of smell. As explained in the previous clairgustance chapter, our extrasensory senses clairalience and clairgustance often go hand in hand as they do in our physical world.

A crucial factor in recognizing when you have a clairalience occurrence, as with all of the other psychic senses, is acknowledging it's different from your physical reality. Sometimes this can be tricky, as we are constantly bombarded with a variety of scents throughout the day. Usually, though, with clairalience there will be no reason for the scent to be present. Anyone who is gifted with receiving psychic knowledge through this clairolfactory sense knows that it can seem as though the scent is really there, stemming from something that's present in their environment; that's how strong it can be. Others who are just beginning to tap into this incredible psychic ability may only catch a passing whiff of the smell and don't always have the acuity to recognize it as an extrasensory scent.

People experiencing clairolfactory scents may pick up on any type of smell, from perfume to cigars, a strong cup of coffee to the stench of burned engine oil, or even dirty diapers to freshly cut flowers. There is nothing off-limits. If you can smell it physically, you will be able to recognize and smell it using your clairalient sense.

Stop and Smell the Roses

So often clairalience presents itself to let us know someone who's passed is with us in spirit. Interestingly enough, this can also be a shared experience. Though no physical scent is there, more than one person may experience it psychically. This happened in a reading with Terri.

"I'm picking up on someone who used to do something with gardening because I'm seeing all different types of shrubbery and greenery," I told her.

"Yes, that would be my uncle. When he was alive, he had his own landscaping business," she replied.

"That makes sense, though it wasn't just lawn cutting or snow plowing. It had to have been, like, architectural landscaping design or something. I'm sensing there's more to it than simply mowing the grass," I continued.

"You're exactly right. He went to school for it! He did only high-end work," she validated.

After her uncle came through, I told her everything else I was getting and she was able to validate it all. We had come to the end of our session and Terri had gotten out her wallet to pay me. All of a sudden, I was overwhelmed by a specific scent.

"Do you smell that?" I asked her. "I smell flowers or perfume."

"Oh. That's funny. Now I'm starting to smell it a little bit," she confirmed.

"I wonder if it's your uncle saying goodbye, you know, with the flowers and everything."

"That would be great! I really smell them now, too!" she added.

"Hmmm. I think there's more to it. I am distinctly smelling roses. Did he used to do a lot of rose planting?" I asked.

"Well, not that I know of …," she answered, thinking.

"I'm also picking up on another smell. It's kind of like old books; I get kind of an old library smell," I continued. "But I still smell the roses as well."

I remained firm in my resolve that I was definitely picking up the scent of roses mixed with old books. She kept busily gathering her belongings, getting ready to leave, not sure if there was any more to the story I was trying to piece together.

"I have to tell you that I'm getting that you need to stop what you're doing and smell the roses. I feel like you're missing someone or forgetting about someone. They are trying to come through for you. They're also making me smell fresh-cut grass and, I can't be sure, but it smells like formaldehyde? They're either referring to the frogs we had to dissect in middle school or maybe the cemetery? And now again, I'm getting a wafting of the roses. This has to mean something to you."

"Holy mother of God! I can't believe I forgot! I went to the cemetery about two weeks ago and put roses on my grandmother's grave! I was hoping she'd come through! I didn't think this was how she'd do it though!" she practically shouted, dropping all of her things to the ground.

"Well, that explains it! But what does the old book smell have to do with it?" I asked.

"She was a librarian a long time ago, before I even knew her, but she used to tell me stories about how the books had a certain scent and she could tell which type of book the patron was about to check out before even looking at them," she answered, now with tears in her eyes. "Amazing. Thanks, Grandma!"

Exercise: Smelling the Roses

Just as Terri's grandmother came through with various scents that were specific to her to let her know she was around, your loved ones from the other side may show up using scents to let you know they are present. For this exercise, it's important that you use not only your physical sense of smell but your extrasensory one as well.

Throughout the day, pay attention to everyone you come in contact with. Smell them, get up real close, and just breathe in their scent. Don't risk, however, that you may be deemed a bit inappropriate by making this too obvious. Make yourself inconspicuous!

Bring your journal with you so you can record whatever scents you pick up on, keeping in mind that this may or may not be the scent that would come through in a reading or a session. The object of this is just to become familiar with the variety of odors people may give off; both good and bad. This gets you used to being open to and understanding what it is you are smelling.

When you are all done for the day, look back over your journal. Do you have any aromas recorded that are similar to each other? Are there any relatives that smell the same? Do people from the same household smell alike? Mark down any similarities as well as any notable differences. Did the results of this exercise surprise you? Or were you not able to make sense of any of it?

A Rose by Any Other Name Would Smell as Sweet

Terri's reading was not unusual. During my sessions, I tend to pick up on people who have passed using all of my senses; this includes my clairalient sense. What was different about her reading was that at first it was a bit confusing because there were overlapping loved ones. I was receiving information about her landscape architect uncle and combining that with my clairescent impression of roses; which, to be honest, made perfect sense. If we hadn't put together the clairalient message of the cemetery, she may never have understood it was her grandmother coming through.

Clairolfaction comes through in other ways as well. The roses I psychically smelled for Terri were based on something literal in that she had actually placed those specific flowers on the gravesite of her deceased grandmother. But psychically smelling roses can have another meaning, too. This I confirmed during another client session.

"I am hoping you are going to connect with my mom," Sherry told me during a reading a few years back.

"I can try. Don't give me too much information, though, I'd rather wait and see what comes through, if anything," I responded.

I was picking up and connecting to many others she had lost, but her mother was eluding me. I wasn't getting anything to connect with her. All I kept smelling were roses. That is often a sign of love or congratulations for me, so I shared that with her.

"Sherry, I'm getting a feeling of someone sending you love. Is there also a reason they'd be congratulating you on something? That's possibly what's coming through as well," I asked her.

"Let me think. I appreciate the love; it's probably from all of the other people you already tuned in to. I don't really know what the congratulations would be for, though. My birthday was about six months ago. My kids' birthdays are a long way off, too. My anniversary was about three months ago. Could that be it?"

"I don't think so. It generally would have to be something closer or something more prevalent. Did you get a promotion or did you get recognized for something at work? I'm grasping at straws here, help me out!" I joked with her.

"Nope! I'd have to say no. I can't think of any reason they'd be singling out to praise me for," she laughed, "other than I'm an incredibly brilliant and beautiful person!"

The scent of roses was not letting up. In fact, it was growing stronger. I just couldn't figure out what it meant. I decided to go with the gardening theme on the off chance I was missing the point.

"Did someone garden a lot? Or were they known for their flowers?" I persevered.

"Not that I'm aware of," she answered, this time with a little less humor. "I really don't understand."

"I'm sorry; it's just that I keep smelling roses. It's becoming so strong it's almost overpowering my physical senses. I don't know what else it could mean. I'm sorry. I'm trying to connect to your mom but I've got nothing. It's not working. Either she's not around right now or I'm just not able to tune in to her," I confessed. I felt bad because I knew that was the main reason Sherry had come to see me.

"Are you kidding me? Leave it to Mom to come through that way. Oh my goodness. You just made me so happy!" Sherry responded with animation.

I was a little baffled. I had just explained that I wasn't able to connect with her mother and here she was excited, convinced I had. Did I overlook something? Was Sherry connecting directly? I didn't get it, and I told her as much.

"Really? I'm sorry, I'm a bit perplexed. Am I missing something? I don't think your mom is coming through," I reiterated.

"Ha ha. Of course she is. You were asking me all of these other questions that made absolutely no logical sense to me. However, you were definitely in tune with her," she replied with a huge, practically glowing smile.

"I don't get it," I said.

"It's her name. It's not what she did, or even anything that I did that would have been deserving of congratulations. Her name was Rose."

After that, everything fell into place. Her mother, Rose, produced all kinds of evidence to let Sherry know she was still part of her life. Later, after Sherry left, I heard the words, "A rose by any other name would smell as sweet." Incredible. I had missed it, but luckily for us, Sherry had not. Rose came through for her in a wonderful way.

Exercise: Smelling the Name and Then Some

Rose showed up by bringing through the scent that represented her name. There are other names that have dual meanings with regard to scent as well.

There are two parts to this exercise. For the first part, open your journal and write down any names you can think of—people that you know or even people that you don't—that obviously share duality with some type of scent. Rose is a great example of this, as is Petunia. You may even know an Autumn.

Remember, last names count as well, so don't discount those.

Next, close your eyes and surround yourself with your protective energy bubble. You want to only let positive energy through for this next part. When you are done, open your eyes and look at the list you've recorded. Try and smell the names. For example, Rose may be a less complex one to start with, provided you know what they smell like. Continue doing this with all of them.

Did you find some scents were easier to psychically pick up on than others? Were you not able to use your clairalience for some? Did some of the smells linger or run into the next name? Make a note of everything you experienced. Though this is primarily a clairalience exercise, you may find that other psychic senses bleed through and bring hits other than the smells. That is okay. You probably have other intuitive gifts that are more prevalent, and those may always take center stage. Feel free to return to this exercise and add additional names.

For the second half of this exercise you are going to try and determine what aroma your friends and family are represented by. This will usually be different than tuning in to what smell people psychically give out, though in some instances it may be the same. Using your journal again, write down people you know or people you are close to, including friends and family both alive and passed. After you've written each name be sure to leave room for notes.

Again, surround yourself with your bubble of protection. Then, one at a time, write down next to each name whatever possible scents you can associate with each individual person. For example, Rose is obvious. Something less obvious may be Peter. But if Peter was a welder by trade, smells of metal or fire may be right on track for him. If Tracy was an emergency room nurse, you may smell antiseptic or other smells associated with hospitals. If your brother is an avid outdoorsman, you may pick up on the scent of the earth or the trees. And if your best friend was a known for her baking, you may enjoy the aroma of freshly made brownies.

The name itself is not always indicative of the fragrance that will come through. Sometimes, it is a particular scent like a cigar or even a perfume. If it has to do with an infant, they may be represented by extreme opposites, such as the unpleasant scent of dirty diapers to the incredible smell of fresh, out-of-the-bath, powdered baby. There is no wrong answer here.

Again record the impressions you've received using your clairalience. Were they all meaningful? Did you think you had a scent to represent someone and then you psychically smelled something else? Were you able to associate a scent with everyone you had written down? Do they all make sense to you? Did you recognize the smells? Did they conjure up any memories or thoughts of the person?

Something Smells Bad

Clairalience is one of those multifaceted intuitive senses. As shown above, it can give you an impression of someone as well as the actual name of someone. This psychic clear smell sense can also transport you to a specific time or event in someone's life or even a location.

Take, for instance, the smell of a local carnival. There may be a mixture of people, oiled machines, fried dough, candy apples, and more. When this type of clairalience comes through, it has no limits. What does it make you think of? It can be a reference to an actual carnival coming to town. It might come up because you or your client truly enjoyed a specific occasion where you went to the carnival and had a great time or something unusual happened. Or, it may just be referencing the carnival atmosphere in general. If someone of great importance to you whom you loved going to carnivals with passed, it may be them trying to come through as well.

Imagine all of the possibilities clairalience presents. The scents may be pleasant in nature, but they may also be noxious or putrid or anything in between. Your clairolfaction does not discriminate. As with clairgustance, the scents you perceive are mainly phantom smells. They are not produced by something that is physically present or that you can smell in reality, rather they are extrasensory or paranormal. However, this obviously doesn't mean that it won't be a real smell.

You receive intuitive impressions from the other side in a way you can understand. Like all of your psychic senses, the universe will provide you only with information that is relatable to your own circumstances or your own life. Clairalience is the same as the others; you will only smell odors you are able to recognize, even if it takes some effort to translate their meaning. Sometimes, unfortunately, the clairalient gifts take you to a place you'd rather not be.

About twenty years ago, I was driving with my mom. We were talking about the probability of my having children at some point in the near future. That led to a discussion about keeping the kids happy and safe. Growing up we didn't have much money, in fact we were quite poor, but I was always happy. My mom, a single parent, was my best friend and I always felt safe. As I got older, our conversations became deeper and more personal but usually stayed on the physical plane versus the paranormal one. This one began light, but quickly turned into something else.

"One of the most important pieces of advice I can give you is as a parent you need to start off the relationship with pure trust. Always have a mutual respect and a mutual trust until or unless they give you a reason not to," she told me.

"I agree. I think that's how it should be with any relationship. Kind of like innocent until proven guilty. Is that how your relationship has always been with Grandmother?" I asked.

"For the most part, yes. There have been a couple of times in my life when I didn't think she believed what I told her or what I felt."

As she was talking, I began to smell a fresh, outdoorsy scent. It smelled like dirt or earth. I had no idea why I smelled it, but I didn't think it was coming from outside of the car. I felt like it was a phantom odor.

"What didn't she believe?" I asked her, the odor becoming stronger.

The aroma of dirt now mixed with manure and hay or straw was wafting through the entire car, though my mother seemed oblivious to it. A smell of stables and horses grew more intense as she continued.

"She didn't believe me when I told her about my lupus diagnosis, but maybe it was because she just didn't want to."

Just then I smelled a barn, and it soon mixed with the scent of sweat and alcohol.

"So, what else was there? I get the distinct impression there's more to it. What are you not telling me?" I pushed her a bit, certain now that there was another story she hadn't told me.

"When I was young, about eleven or twelve, my friend and I used to go riding at the stables."

I was beginning to understand the phantom scent I smelled.

"There was this man there; he took care of the horses. He always smelled like sweat and booze. I don't think anything actually happened to my friend, and I know it didn't to me, but he was very inappropriate. He was always making comments and looking at us with a lascivious grin. He tried to lure me into the barn by myself one day, and after that I never went back. I told my mom about it and my friend told her parents, but I don't think they ever believed us. I always wondered what happened to him and if he ever hurt any other kids," she shared. "I've never told anyone else about that," she confessed with a far-off look in her eyes.

I recognized the smell of horses and stables because there was a riding camp near my home. By not jumping to the conclusion that it was specifically about horse camp (since that was my personal experience) I was able to stay open to receiving more, like the sweat and alcohol scent. Thankfully, my mother was not harmed and relied on her own intuition to keep her safe. Without trying, my clairalient abilities easily picked up on the situation, likely because we were so close and I sensed her danger at the time.

Exercise: What's That Smell?

Again, there are two parts to this exercise.

If you can, remember an occasion when your clairalient sense popped up, out of the blue, possibly during a discussion with someone or at an event, and record it in your journal. Try and remember every detail about what you were doing, whom you were with, and when it was. Then, write down whatever scents you picked up on. Did you smell something familiar? Was it something you recognized? Did it make you jump to a conclusion about what it was? Or what it was in reference to? Were you able to accurately determine what it meant? Or whom it was about? Write everything down. Answer any other questions you may be able to think up regarding this clairalient experience.

Was this the first time you'd ever had a clairalient impression? If not, go ahead and write that one down, too. Be sure, again, to record all of the details.

The second part of this exercise involves using your clairolfactory sense to learn from what you have in your memory bank. Think back to an event or something different from your normal, everyday activities. It might have been a vacation to somewhere on the ocean or it may have been your last sporting event. It may just have been a trip to a local carnival. Whatever it was, begin focusing on the memory of it.

Now, what do you smell? Close your eyes and remember being there. What did it smell like? Were there multiple scents? Can you pick apart each one? Did you like the smell? Was it sweet? Sour? Dirty? Clean? Does the scent seem familiar? Does it surprise you? Does it smell how you imagine it would? Record every detail. Was it easy to tune in to your clairalient sense when you used your memory? Or was it difficult? When you think you've experienced every aroma, think about it one more time. Do you smell anything else? Write it all down.

Next, compare both situations. Did the time you had a clairolfactory experience come to mind more easily than remembering an event and trying to turn on your clairalience? Or vice versa? Which felt better? Which was more comfortable? Feel free to go back and compare anything else you've written down for similarities as well as differences.

Yum, Yum, Good

Not everything that comes through that smells good will make you feel good. As shown by my clairalient tuning in to the stables from my mother's childhood, the smell of horses did not evoke feelings of joy. Unfortunately, there were bad memories attached to a very fresh smell. Sometimes, thankfully, clairolfactory impressions that are pleasant may indeed bring to mind cheerful thoughts that actually represent times of happiness.

People who have passed will try and make their presence known. They will generally use whatever means possible in order to do this. For instance, your uncle who was known for smoking pipes may send through to you the scent of his favorite tobacco. Or, your sister might send through the smell of the old bedroom you shared growing up. Or, you may smell the odor of peach schnapps that reminds you of the last night you spent with your best friend before she died and who's got a sense of humor even in death—that peach schnapps tasted much better going down than it did on its way back up!

My father-in-law stopped smoking cigarettes and started smoking cherry mini cigars in an effort to cut back on the nicotine, which unfortunately was a little too late as he died from what began as throat cancer. Every once in a while, my husband and I will both smell those cherry cigars and we will know he's visiting. My mother-in-law comes through smelling like perfume. Not because she liked to wear it. Actually, she never wore makeup or perfume. Her name was Rosemary, so we always smell rose perfume whenever she's around. We are lucky in that my husband and I are able to validate each other's clairalience because we both receive the same psychic impressions.

Not knowing someone's loved ones from the other side helps me as a professional psychic medium to tune in to their deceased relatives in a very organic and clean way. Using my clairolfaction, as well as my other psychic senses, I'm able to pick up and bear witness to the scents they are sending without having any previous knowledge of their lives. This keeps me open to anything I may pick up. And it leaves me entirely free from any judgment about just what is coming through. I have no bias and no opinion about the information I receive—usually.

Deenah came in to see me one day. She wanted to know what I picked up on and whether I was able to tune in to any of her family members. We discussed a lot. We talked about her job at a nonprofit business and we talked about her possibly selling her house and moving somewhere else. I was able to clarify some of her questions and also raise some new ones.

"I'm getting the aroma of someone doing some Middle Eastern cooking. I'm not sure of the specific spices, but it is making me feel like it's the Mideast. Does this make sense to you? I'm also picking up on the scent of multiple people, women I think, from your family who are cooking with you together in the kitchen," I told her.

"That makes perfect sense. We used to get together for the holidays and such and cook. My family is Middle Eastern, and we cooked like that on occasion," Deenah answered.

"Hmmm. I am smelling a specific flavor that I believe your grandmother is taking credit for. I can't tell you what the name of the spices are, but for some reason they are significant in this dish," I continued.

"Yes, you are absolutely right. My grandmother was the glue that kind of held everyone together in the kitchen. We used her recipes when we cooked together!" Deenah confirmed.

"Okay, but there is something more. I smell an almost overwhelming scent of herbs, and I feel like your grandmother is trying to tell you something or show you something," I went on to explain.

"That's because she taught me how to dry fresh herbs, and we used to do that together!" Deenah replied, smiling.

This clairalient experience was definitely a pleasant one. Even though I personally can't eat a lot of the spices in Middle Eastern-style cooking, I was able to recognize them, which brought some comfort to Deenah. This was an activity she fondly remembered sharing with her deceased loved one. Her grandmother sent me these overpowering aromas to let Deenah know she was there.

Loved ones come through with a myriad of cooking smells. More often than not, if someone liked to cook or was known for their family meals, they will send those particular scents to us so we'll know they are saying hello. This happened during my client Mindy's session as well.

"This is kind of interesting. I'm hearing, 'It's not gravy.' I smell pasta sauce. I used to date someone who was part of a very Italian family, and they had the big Italian meals every weekend. They'd make a big pot of sauce and have it boiling on the stove all day. They called it their Sunday gravy. I always joked with them that it was pasta sauce. I told them gravy is what you put on turkey! I'm getting this same aroma; the smell of a big pot of sauce," I told her. "Is this your grandmother?"

"Wow. Yup. That'd be her. And we call it sauce, too! We are Italian, but it's always been sauce, not gravy!" she replied.

The smell of cooking food for many is a comforting one. It evokes memories of family meals shared and holidays spent together around the table. It calls to mind feelings of love, and sometimes discord, but family nonetheless. The clairalient gift that allows us to bring forth those memories is a precious one. It is this same gift that can remind us of our weekly rituals in the kitchen or the times we spent with our grandparents or the cooking we did every night with our spouse. Tuning in to our clairescence in this way makes us feel good.

Exercise: What's Cooking?

Go somewhere comfortable where you'll be undisturbed for at least half an hour. Then, take a nice deep breath. Close your eyes. Imagine that all around you the air is beginning to fill with pure oxygen, making it much easier to breathe. With every breath you begin to feel more relaxed, more at peace, more calm. Continue breathing this way until your limbs start to feel almost as though they are no longer attached.

When this happens, you are ready. Take another deep breath and imagine your childhood home. Don't tune in to the people there, just the home itself. Now, specifically imagine yourself in the kitchen. As you look around take note of what you see. Do you recognize the stove? The refrigerator? Possibly a table or chairs? What else is there? A sink? Cabinets? Whatever there is pay attention to the colors, shape, and design of everything. Allow yourself to be transported back in time.

Once you feel you've truly landed in the middle of your kitchen from your childhood, it's time to get to work. What smells can you imagine coming from this kitchen? Did you cook in here? Did your mother? Your father? Your sister? Your brother? Your grandparents? Aunts or uncles? Try and only tune in to the aromas coming from the kitchen.

Do you smell ethnic foods such as Italian sauce bubbling on the stove or Spanish rice and beans cooking in a pot? How about pierogi like you used to make with your Polish side of the family or the braised lamb you cooked with the Greek side?

If you grew up like me, you may smell basic foods that tend to cross cultures such as chili, beef stew, beef goulash, elbow noodles with Ragu and hot dogs, or even disgusting tuna casserole (sorry, Mom!). It doesn't matter what type of food it is. What matters is that you tune in to whatever foods you remember or whatever smells you remember emanating from that childhood kitchen.

If, instead of fond thoughts, all you can remember by being in the kitchen of your childhood home are harsh memories, imagine going somewhere you had a pleasant cooking or food experience. This is about calling up happy and safe memories.

Once you've recognized and can indeed smell at least two distinct flavors, try and determine who, specifically, is attached to those flavors. Is it one of your parents or grandparents? Your siblings? Extended relatives? Or friends? Perhaps you lived in a boarding school or a foster home. Tune in to any of the food odors there as well. It doesn't matter where it is, only that you are able to understand and smell the aromas.

When you've identified everyone attached to the foods, take a few deep breaths and open your eyes. Then, get out your journal and open it to a fresh page. At the top write "Clairescence Cooking from Childhood." Then, list all of the smells you can remember or experienced during this exercise as well as the people you were able to associate with them.

Are the people you've tagged still here? Are they alive or dead? Were you surprised by any of the names that popped up? Or did you expect them all? Were there any who have passed whom you've felt around you before? Or was this the first time they came to mind? Was there a specific event or experience associated with what you tuned in to? If so, what was it? And did it involve multiple people?

Write down everything you can remember and take a minute or two to go over it and reread it. Smell it and see if it feels right.

I Smell a Rat

The scents you smell with clairolfaction represent, for the most part, real events, locations, or people both alive and passed. Clairescence affords you the opportunity of connecting with more than just your psychic eyes or ears and can give you the same amount of information, if not more. Clairalience can also help you smell when things are off or when something's not quite right.

Have you ever had the feeling that what was happening around you was wrong, but you couldn't put your finger on what it was? Or you were about to do something but it didn't feel like a good idea? That's what this type of clairalience is. It is that "something smells off" kind of feeling. It's a warning that you need to heed your intuitive sense, which is telling you to steer clear of the situation you are contemplating or are up against.

Marcy came in for a reading. She had a nervous energy that I wasn't totally understanding, but I knew there was something going on. Sometimes when clients come in they are just nervous so their energy is somewhat scattered. Without giving it too much thought, because I knew whatever needed to come through in the reading would, I began the session. She was looking to connect to the other side and talk to her mother who had passed. She wasn't prepared for what her mother had to tell her, however.

"She wants you to know that she's not in pain anymore. The cancer is gone. She's saying you can stop worrying," I told her.

"Oh, that's wonderful! That's what I wanted to know. I just had to make sure. Now I feel like I can move on," Marcy answered.

"Hmmm, about that. I smell a rat," I said.

My clairalient sense was kicking in. Something smelled off to me. I was picking up a rancid smell that was telling me there was a bad situation or someone was being dishonest in Marcy's life.

"No. I had a feeling you were going to bring this up. I was afraid I was right. Ugh. I didn't want to deal with this right now. I've got too much on my plate," she responded, clearly dejected and exhausted from the possibility of the situation.

"I'm sorry, but it sounds like you already know. Just because I'm verifying it for you doesn't mean you have to do anything about it. It's your choice," I told her, wondering if we were talking about the same thing.

"Before I jump to any conclusions, what is it you're picking up on?"

"Marcy, I think this is a situation that's been going on for a while now. It's about your husband. He's having an affair, and unfortunately it's not the first time," I confessed to her. I smelled a nasty smell, which changed to a different foul smell, letting me know it was more than one person.

One look at her face and I knew she was aware.

"I'm sorry, but your mom is sending me the smell of autumn, which means that is when you will have to make a decision about your relationship. She will help you," I explained. "That will give you almost a year."

"Great. Thanks. At least I know I don't have to deal with it right away," Marcy said with a smile. "Right now there's just too much going on."

Even though Marcy didn't want to deal with her marriage at the moment, she was glad her mother was looking out for her and giving her a time frame. I smelled a rat because her mom sent me the smell. I was able to interpret it for Marcy to understand what her mother wanted to tell her. She was even able to set apart for me more than one foul odor so I would know there was more than just one indiscretion.

There are other reasons something may not smell right. Imagine contemplating a new business venture but every time you think about it you smell a rank odor. Or you've been asked out on a date by someone you just met but you can't stop smelling a fetid scent. Now, take it a step further to the future outcome of the above situations. That new business you were going to join in went under within a couple of months. The person you were supposed to date just got arrested for domestic violence. These clairalient experiences saved you from having troubles down the road. Would you have heeded the messages of caution your psychic senses were sending you? Or would you have ignored them?

I had another client, Nicole, who asked me what I thought of her working for a friend who was getting their business off the ground. Before she said anything else, I began smelling a putrid smell. I knew if Nicole went to work for that person it would not end well. She believed, nevertheless, that it would pay off. She then told me she would be working for free in the beginning, but she would get paid once the company began making money.

Now, I'm a big proponent of helping people out but I also believe you shouldn't work for free. There is too much resentment, and it rarely turns out the way you think it will, especially when you are working for a friend. That's exactly what I was afraid of—that it would end badly.

"I don't feel like it's a good idea. I honestly don't think you'll ever get paid, and I'm getting that you are being strung along. I smell something foul in the air regarding it," I explained. "I know you are all hoping for the best, but it's not going to take off. In other words, it won't work and you'll end up unhappy with the situation."

She didn't listen to me, but that's okay. She had her own path to travel. She also believed it would blossom into a great business. After all, it did have potential. But unfortunately, I was right. It hasn't amounted to much financially, and Nicole, after working for about eight months for free, never saw a dime but was expected to work hard. Needless to say, it didn't end well.

It's not unheard of, this smelling thing that we know as clairalience. In fact, it's more common than you'd imagine. It's about recognizing it. When you smell something bad, such as a skunk, you assume it's an actual material smell. It's hard to differentiate at times between your clairalience and your physical sense of smell.

These knowing smells can also be present for something good. They are not limited to always being harbingers of bad news. You may smell candy canes or evergreens when asking at what point you are going to get a hold of your finances to let you know Christmas is going to be a good time of year. Or, you may smell coffee to let you know if you should meet a friend in the morning. You might also smell "success" when asking if the college major you are choosing will be a good one. This smell of success may be a combination of all of your favorite scents or it may be an invigorating or even a sweet scent. This aroma is not going to be the same for everyone—you are unique, therefore your scent for success will also be one of a kind, personalized to you.

Exercise: Turn That Frown Upside Down

Having the clairalient message to know when you should think twice about becoming involved with someone or something is a handy gift to have. Recognizing your bouquet for success is also a useful tool. But what happens when you put them both together? You create the ability to change an event from something that may have been negative to something positive. Before you can do that, you need to discover what each smells like, specifically for you.

Close your eyes. Take a nice deep breath and relax. As you continue breathing, imagine you have a warm, golden cloak spreading over your shoulders and down over your body. This cloak will protect you and keep you safe from anything you don't want invading your energetic space while also feeding your power. Imagine this cloak is very comfortable and charged with a positive energy that is going to help you interpret your smell of success.

On the next long deep breath, feel your golden cloak wrapping comfortably around you. As it does, you begin to smell a wonderful, wafting aroma spreading around you. This scent is the smell of success. Notice what it smells like. Is it sweet? Fruity? Does it have the tinge of metal? Is it powerful? Does it smell invigorating? Minty? Allow the cloak to help magnify the smell even more. Did that change the scent? Did it make it stronger? More fresh? Once you are sure you have the smell of success, go ahead and open your eyes and write it down in your journal. Describe it as completely as possible. You will be tuning in to that scent again.

Now, close your eyes again. Think back to a time when you weren't happy with a situation or a person or how something turned out. How did it make you feel? It could have been something really bad or it may have been something just very off-putting. Whatever it was, tune in to it now. Call in your clairalience. What does this event or person smell like to you? Does it make you feel nauseated or disgusted? Is it a gross scent? Try and smell it as strongly as possible, letting the acrid odor permeate your psychic nostrils.

Once you've gotten to the point that it is so strong you almost can't take it anymore, wrap it in the golden cloak and allow yourself to smell the scent of success from before. Imagine your powerful cloak wrapping around the bad situation and making it feel better to you. This does not mean that it will change the outcome of the previous event, but it will allow you in the future to adjust a situation merely by creating a shift in the energy. This will be very helpful when you have a bad aroma surrounding something that you actually have to do or someone you have to be with.

Now, try and smell the bad or nasty scent again. Does it smell any better? Can you smell success around it? If so, great! If not, wrap it in the golden cloak again. Do this with future events that you must be part of in order to change the energy from negative to positive.

Not Everyone Smells the Same Thing

I find that I'm always asking my husband, "Do you smell that?" Whether it has to do with my car, our dogs, the house, clothing, or even at the movies, I realize he doesn't always smell what I smell. This, I believe, is because I am using not only my physical sense of smell, or smelling something externally, I am also utilizing my clairalient abilities. He doesn't smell the same things; I'm experiencing these scents psychically. Determining whether the scent is external or internal will help you in understanding whether you are tapping into your intuition and need to pay attention to something. Always use your gifts and smell the sweetness life has to offer.

eight

Clairtangency (Clear Touch)

"If only all the hands that reach could touch."
—MARY LOBERG

H old out your hand," I said to my student Kelly.

I was teaching a workshop called Developing Your Intuition and, as is my norm, all of the students were there for hands-on practice. We had been working on meditation and tuning in to our auras and chakras all morning. We'd also connected to our other psychic senses, which had some people excelling more than others. So far there'd been a lot of laughter as well as a strong amount of doubt over being able to actually read anyone. Most of the people in the class knew that everyone was intuitive, but they didn't necessarily believe they'd be able to tune in to each other or receive any type of messages. They wanted the quick and easy version of using their psychic senses. So, I gave it to them!

"I'm going to place an object in your palm, and I want you to try and tune in to the energy of it. What do you pick up about the object? How does it make you feel?" I continued asking Kelly questions, instructing her to keep her eyes closed.

"Don't judge the information that is coming through. Just say it out loud and I will write down whatever you say," I let her know.

She started to grumble, but I told her it didn't matter what she got in the moment. We were all there to practice and it was a safe environment. What mattered was that she tried. She needed to believe enough in the possibility of psychic ability that she could be open to the process.

We were working with psychometry. Psychometry is based on the principle that all objects hold energy and that energy can be tuned in to when you hold or touch the object. Metal objects and pictures tend to hold the most energy. The impressions you receive can be garnered through all of your psychic senses. Usually, accessing clear feeling is the initial step to opening your awareness. This extraordinary sense is more readily available through touch or clairtangency.

"I can't quite figure out what this means, but I guess I feel kind of happy and excited about it," she said.

Her first foray into clairtangency was right on. I asked her more questions.

"Where do you think it came from? Was it a gift? How was it made? What is it?" I continued with a barrage of rapid-fire questions.

"Ha ha. I don't know!" she answered with a nervous laugh.

"Take them one at a time. Where do you think it came from?"

"I feel like it's somewhere warm and dry. Maybe California or New Mexico?"

"All right. Was it a gift or was it purchased?"

"I feel like the person who owns this wanted it and got it on the spot," she meekly responded, almost as if asking a question.

"Great. And was it handmade? Made in a factory? How did it come to be?"

"I feel hands all over it, so I'd have to say it was handmade."

"And what is it?"

"I'm getting bracelet? I think it has turquoise or something because it feels almost like Native American. I don't know. Can I look yet?" She was getting excited now.

"Almost. What does it mean to the owner? Is it special or is it just something they had laying around? Does it mean anything?" I was trying to get as much as possible out of her.

"I think it's special. It almost represents a turning point in her life or something. Is it yours? Can I look?" she wanted to know.

"Yes, you can look!"

When all was said and done, Kelly was able to tune in to the energy of the bracelet I had placed in her hand with her previously unrecognized clairtangent abilities. She talked about who had made it, what type of stones were present in it, what it meant to me, and more. I validated everything for her. It was mine, and I had gotten it in Arizona. It was made by Native Americans, and it was silver and turquoise. It meant a lot to me because I purchased it on the first retreat I led in Arizona; that was definitely a turning point. Though Kelly was not 100 percent accurate with everything, she was pretty darn close!

She was surprised that this exercise in psychometry helped her to tune in to her psychic abilities. Though she was not entirely pleased that she hadn't excelled with her other intuitive senses, she was very happy that her clairtangency was kicking in.

Exercise: Psychometry

Gather some friends together and ask everyone to bring an object. Get some paper and pens—enough for all of you to do multiple writings. Place all of the items in a bag without looking and pick one. Hold the object in your hands for a least a minute and then write down whatever you pick up about it.

How does it feel in your hand? Is it vibrating or moving or still? Does it feel hot or warm or cool or freezing? Is it old or new? Do you get any names or initials with it? Do you pick up on any locations? Do you feel any colors? Does it feel like male or female energy? Do you feel any specific person attached to it, such as grandmother, husband, sister, friend, etc.? Is it an important item? Was it given to the person as a gift or did they buy it themselves? Was it passed down through generations?

Now tune in to the owner directly. How is the overall mood of the person who owns it? Are they happy? Are they sad? Are they depressed? Are they excited? What else do you pick up about them? Do they work? Do they have children? Are they married? What do they do on a regular basis? Do you feel anyone around them from the other side? Are they comfortable? Are they financially secure?

Write down anything else you may get about the object or the person or people surrounding the object. Be sure to include even the smallest details. Remember, just because you may not understand what you are feeling doesn't mean they won't. What you pick up and know nothing about may mean the world to them!

Not Just Objects

Many people experience clairtangency through psychometry, but the two terms are not interchangeable. Psychometry is the reading of an object or a picture by holding it in your hand, which is a form of clairtangency. There is more fun to be had with clairtangency, however! Clairtangency, or clear touch, is also productive when touching actual people.

We are all made up of energy. Every living thing as well as every object is made of energy. Energy is essentially the capacity of a system that does work or the action of actually being at work. Psychic energy is the same thing, but it is more specific to the psychic aspect as opposed to the physical. It is this energy that we send out to the world that others can pick up on. It is also this energy that makes up our aura.

Our aura is our etheric or energetic body that surrounds us and emanates from us. Often depicted as halos or aureoles on pictures of saints, our aura actually flows out of and around every part of us. Auras change constantly based on our ever-changing moods and our physical well-being. It is also where we are able to create the energy to heal ourselves—body, mind, and spirit. In their book *The Healing Power of Your Aura,* Martin and Moraitis write about the curative abilities that take place in the aura, "The aura is a crucial part of healing because the aura is the place where you generate the spiritual energy to manifest health." (Martin and Moraitis, 2006)

Radiating auric energy carries messages as well as healing properties. It sends out currents of information that the universe is able to detect and we are able to read through touch or clairtangency. Imagine all of our physical, emotional, mental, and spiritual characteristics, maladies, and joys streaming out of us like radio waves and these undulating torrents carry information that can be tuned in to. Well, it can.

Let's look to the movies. The portrayal of psychics in many movies is shown by the gypsy woman with the wavy black hair, laden with scarves, a round table between her and her client, and a crystal ball or cards displayed on the tablecloth. Usually, the lights are dimmed, the atmosphere is a bit spooky, and the reader is intense. This can all be true, and you may have been to someone whose reading area is set up this way! Take it one step further; what often comes next is the holding of the hands. The fortuneteller asks to hold the sitter's hand. Not always to read the palm, but just to get energy off of the actual person through touch.

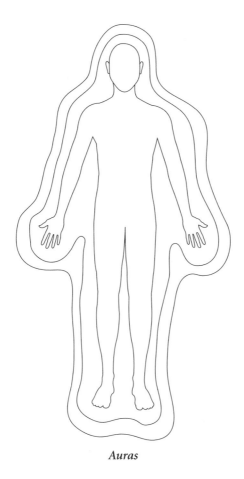

Auras

The occasional misconception that this is how all psychics or intuitives work has some validity. This clairtangent gift, though not always like it is in the movies, is one way to get information and messages from and for a person. I often have people ask me when they sit down in my chair across from my desk, "Do you need to hold my hands or something?" after they've warmed them by rubbing them together.

They are not too far off. Sometimes if I have a client that I'm having a difficult time tuning in to, I will do a very quick one- to two-minute meditation and then I will have them lay their hands on mine. I think it's a mix of the supposed ritual and the clairtangency that opens the client's energy in order for me to then tune in to them. Sometimes it feels almost electric.

I recently held a large gallery event where about 130 people came hoping to connect in some way to their deceased loved ones, whom I affectionately call dead people. I had tuned in to a whole bunch of spirits from the other side, ranging from children to grandparents, and they just kept banging on the door wanting to come in. This, of course, is great. It meant I was able to read for a lot of people.

"I have an S name," I told the audience. I usually get initials right off the bat, and then comes the evidence and the rest of the name. "I feel like it's for someone in this area."

At that, I had about four different groups claiming the S name.

"I think it's Stephen," I continued.

Still, two or three people were staking their claims to the reading.

"It's me," said one in particular. "I had a Stephen who's passed."

Now, normally I don't recall most of my readings. This was no different. I don't remember what I told her, only that Stephen was coming through with verifiable information. Throughout my reading for that particular person, someone in the back of the room kept pointing to her friend. Melissa, whom I couldn't identify at the time, said, "I think it's for us."

"Hmmm. I think you're right, and I want to give you Stephen, but I can't quite grasp what he's telling me," I told them honestly.

During the rest of the gallery event, I kept going back to that little group at the back of the room. "I know Stephen is here for you, and I know he wants me to talk to you, but I just am not getting anything else from him!"

The end of the event was upon us, and people were laughing and crying right up to the conclusion. Many had gotten a sense of peace and wanted to thank me. I was hugging and talking and hugging some more until most of the people had moved on. I was making my way to the book-signing table when Stephen's people walked up to me. I recognized Melissa, but I didn't recognize the two men. I had no idea if one was her husband or what the dynamic was until afterward.

I shook Eric's hand, and then it started. "You are the one Stephen wanted to relay a message to," I said.

"Yes," he replied simply.

"He was your partner and he died of AIDS," I continued.

"Yes," he smiled.

"He wants you to know he loves you still and approves of your brand-new union," I said.

He smiled again.

"This is your new partner," I said, motioning toward the other man there.

He nodded.

"There's more to it. He wants to bless your new union. He's very happy for you and he approves," I continued, almost trancelike.

I knew it wasn't just another boyfriend. There was more to it. Stephen was telling me there was more to it.

"We just got married on Sunday," Eric replied, and the tears of joy welled up in all of our eyes.

I hadn't been able to connect to Stephen to properly channel his message to Eric and his new husband during the gallery. I wasn't able to share his love until I shook Eric's hand. The turning point was the contact. Through psychic touch, or clairtangency, I connected to their energy. I'm glad, as I'm sure Eric is, that he took the couple of minutes to stay after the event. The only regret I have is I wasn't able to share it with the entire gallery to amplify the love we felt coming through in that moment. Though I fully believe Stephen wanted his own private ceremony.

Clairtangency and clairsentience (see chapter 4) sometimes go hand in hand, pun intended! Clairtangency is the ability to read someone or something by touching them. Clairsentience allows you to feel things about someone or something. Clairtangency can evoke those feelings while in contact with an object or a person as well. Your touching sense also involves clairvoyance and clairaudience. Touch is the means by which you're able to connect, but you still need to receive the information. Your other clairs help out with that.

Exercise: Reach Out and Touch Someone

Invite friends over. It has to be at least five people. Make sure you tell them ahead of time that they will be part of a psychic exercise! Invoke your circle of white light of protection around you before you start. You want to be sure only positive energy is allowed to come through.

Then, in a separate room, put two chairs facing each other and turn the light off. Close your eyes, blindfold them even, and sit in one of the chairs. Have each friend come in, one at a time. Have them sit down in the chair across from you. Put your hands out, palms down. Have them lay their hands gently on yours, light enough so you won't recognize them, but heavy enough so you can feel their presence.

Begin telling the person sitting there everything you pick up on. It doesn't matter how you receive the information. You may hear, see, feel, taste, or smell details about them. Try not to discount anything you receive. Just share it as you get it.

Have each person quietly leave the room and write down everything you told them. Then, do the same thing for the next person. After you are done with all of your friends, have them read over what they wrote down. Did any of it make sense to them? Did it not? How did it feel to you? Did it feel good?

Did it feel bad? Scary? Exciting? Did it feel natural to you to read people when you were touching their hands? Was it helpful?

Mix it up a little bit. Have someone else take a turn with the blindfold on. How do they do? Are they accurate? How did it feel having someone else read you?

Compare notes with all of your friends. Did anything stand out when you read someone that also came up when someone else read for them? Was everything different?

My New Bed

Furniture is a gateway to psychic messages. It holds energy just as much if not more than other objects and pictures. Just imagine everything an old dining room table has to tell you—the stories it could share. Think about all of the meals spent there with family and friends. Kick it up a notch and envision all of the holidays spent around the table. Now picture the games played there and the homework done every day while eating the afterschool snack. There may have been dinner parties and victory celebrations or even school meetings held around that same table. Just imagine.

Furniture also gets passed down from generation to generation. Now all of those activities have just doubled, even tripled, with each new family. Consider all of the energy that's surrounded and passed through that table. Now, reflect on how much more there would be if you bought the table at an antique shop! The potential energy is endless.

Frances learned about the possibilities quite by accident. She called me one day, years ago, because she wanted to come in and have a reading. She was positive she was being haunted, but she couldn't figure out for the life of her who it could be. She knew she had lost a few people, but they were quite distant from her. She didn't think there was any reason any of them would have come back to bother her. I asked her to meet me in my office for a session.

"I can't take it anymore. I don't understand why this is happening or what exactly is going on," Frances told me.

"I'm sorry you are having such a hard time. Let's see if we can determine what is happening. "

I began tuning in to her energy and started picking up images involving her bedroom and nighttime.

"Are you having trouble sleeping? Are you being awakened? I'm getting the feeling that every night when you go to bed it begins. Is this what's happening?" I asked her.

"Yes, and I can't take it anymore! I swear it's making me nuts. With the lack of sleep and the feeling of dead people all around me, it's making me insane!"

"Okay. I'm getting the feeling it started about six months ago. Does this make sense?" I could feel the change in the atmosphere of the house.

"Hmmm. I think so. Now that you're saying that, it makes total sense. What does it mean?" Frances questioned.

She had a look of sheer desperation in her eyes. It was obvious there was no way she was going to make it through this. I had to figure out a way to help her before she lost her mind.

"I'm picking up that you are very intuitive. Are you aware of this?" I asked.

"Well, I always thought I had something but never did I think I was psychic," she responded.

"Your psychic senses have been kind of jump-started over the past six months. Something has caused this, and I think I know what it is. Are you seeing an older man, white hair, gray beard? He's tall and thin. And a woman, a bit shorter and thicker around the middle with a white night-gown?"

"Oh my God! Yes! How did you know? That's exactly what I get!"

"You recently acquired a new bedroom set, didn't you? An antique?"

"That's right…"

"About six months ago?"

"Yes, I … oh my goodness. Wait. What does this mean?"

"It means you are experiencing a haunting, though not a malevolent one. I feel like this is a residual thing. The bed you are sleeping on belonged to this older couple. They are still there, repeating their nightly rituals over and over again. You are caught in a residual haunting pattern. They are not there to hurt you, and honestly I don't even feel they are aware of you," I explained.

"Then why am I connecting to them if they don't even know I'm there?"

"You are tuning in using clairtangency. Every time you get in bed you are 'touching' their lives. It's through this psychic sense of touch that you are linking to their energy. I hate to say this, but you either have to do some kind of cleansing or, if that doesn't work, you need to get rid of the bed. I think that's their attachment. The rest of their old, your new, furniture is all right. You're very good at tuning in using your clairtangent sense, so this won't stop until you clear it. I'm sorry, but just know that this is not anything that will harm you. You can specifically try asking them to move on, go to the light, but because it's residual it may need a good smudging. That alone may be enough to clear their energy and let you reclaim your new bed!"

"All right. At least I know now what's going on. I thought I was totally losing it. My husband thought I was losing it. And I was cranky all the time from lack of sleep. Thank you so much!" Frances said, happy to finally have answers.

I explained to Frances that she could buy sage locally and burn it around the bed and even blow the smoke under the bed. This would help her, I explained, to clear the residual energy from the old couple that was living out their nightly rituals over and over again.

I heard back from her a few weeks later. She had bought the sage and cleared her bedroom, especially her bed. She was very excited to tell me she was now sleeping. No more waking up and staying awake all night. Though she obviously was still connecting through her clairtangent gifts, she wasn't losing sleep anymore. The couple had moved on and so had she. She, actually, was now trying to tune in using her clairtangent gifts. She regularly tuned in to random objects to see what she could get. She shared that sometimes she had no idea whether she was accurate because there was no way to get feedback, but she felt she was more on point than off. Indeed, I agreed with her.

As Frances found out, antique furniture holds a lot of energy, especially residual energy. For some people, it can be very taxing and can create a hardship, or it can be very interesting. For others, it doesn't affect them at all and they don't even notice it. It all depends on their level of clairtangent ability. If they are fluent with their psychic sense of touch, they may only have to pick up or touch the object for it to transport them to a different dimension. Others may not quite understand exactly what it is they are tuning in to, as happened with Frances. She knew she was seeing or experiencing something, but she couldn't pinpoint exactly what it was until I helped her.

Exercise: Go Antiquing!

Think of this exercise as a field trip! You are going to have to leave your home. You can start out with any antiques you may have in your house, but you should look at this as an opportunity to pick up energy from other families instead of your own.

Bring a friend to an antique shop. Surround yourself and your friend with the circle of protection before you begin. Then, one at a time, begin touching objects, taking a moment to tune in clairtangently before letting go. Write down everything you pick up on. After you're finished, have your friend do the same. Continue doing this with at least five different objects. Try and do this with older items—chances are these objects will carry more of a history. Compare what you've written down afterward, but before leaving the store so you have the opportunity to check out the antiques.

Does what you've written down jive with what your friend recorded? Or was it completely different? Are you able to validate anything by looking at any of the tags or labels attached to the objects? Can you verify anything with the store owner or clerk? How much, if anything, did you get about each object? How did it feel? Did any of the objects make you uncomfortable? Did they make you feel good? Or happy? Or sad? Did you feel as though you were lucky to be touching them? Was it simple? Was it difficult?

Overall, did this form of clairtangency feel comfortable? Practice this again at different stores. Also, try it with other items such as cars and playground swings. The only problem is you won't be able to get validation, but you will be able to practice tuning in and it will help you learn how you receive the information.

Nope, I'm Not Wearing That

Clairtangence is about touching, so it follows suit that coming into contact with fabric or articles of clothing can also send out information that you may be able to tune in to. This psychic sense can give you clues about many things, including the people who made the fabric, the person who sold it to you or gave it to you, or even the person who owned it before you.

Growing up with a single mother, it seemed we were always counting pennies. At times, that meant my mom would sew clothes for me. This also meant we would shop at a thrift store instead of the mall. I didn't mind that much, except it sometimes created an argument or at least a frustrating conversation. We'd go shopping and I'd try on clothes and my mom would love them.

"That looks fantastic on you!" she'd exclaim.

"I can't stand it," I'd say.

"But it really looks great!" she'd insist.

"It doesn't feel good," I'd tell her.

This happened often. It didn't matter how good the clothing looked on me, if it didn't feel right to me I didn't want it. It wasn't just about the fabric; there was more to it. Some clothing made me feel yucky and some made me feel ill. Others would make me feel like I wanted to run screaming out of the store. This was not a normal reaction that anyone seemed to have, but I did, on a regular basis. At the time, I didn't understand what that meant.

I was experiencing clairtangent vibes as a child, although I had no idea that's what it was. My mom, try as she might, would actually buy the clothes, insisting I'd change my mind because they "looked so nice on me," but they'd sit at the back of my closet, never to be worn. Other clothes felt good, and luckily looked okay on me, so those were the ones I stuck to. I still remember my red and white checked pants—I know, sounds over the top now but they felt perfect to me then. They made me happy.

Many girlfriends will commandeer their boyfriend's sweatshirts to wear to bed because it "feels" like their boyfriend, which feels good to them. They are tuning in to them through their clairtangent sense. Used clothing, shoes, and jewelry all have a tendency to hold on to energy more than new items—particularly because someone else has worn the new (old) stuff before you. The mental and physical state of the previous owner can still be attached. Think of the phrase "wearing your heart on your sleeve." That is more accurate than most people know. The energy of the last person who wore the object is still attached.

Not all clothing or jewelry will hold energy that can be felt. Often, it is the special articles of clothing that will carry the emotions and even the personality of the person who used to wear them. Items such as college sweatshirts or even college rings hold energy. Definitely highly emotional items such as wedding dresses or wedding rings exude energy. Depending on the mental or emotional state of the person when they wore them last, these objects may feel good or bad or anything in between. And if you're psychically in tune to your clairtangent abilities, you will most likely pick up on the energy.

Exercise: You Wear It Well

Again, protect yourself with the sphere of protection. This is important because you are specifically trying to tune in to someone else's energy and wear it. Now, do the same thing you did with the antiques, but this time go to a thrift shop. Next, pick out some clothing that you can try on.

Give each article at least a couple of minutes on your body. How does it feel? Do you like it? Do you not like it? Try and look past the way it physically looks on your body and feel whether it has good energy or bad, whether it makes you happy or sad. If it makes you feel good, buy it! We can all use an extra injection of happiness!

Medical Intuition

Maybe one of the most important uses for clairtangency is medical intuition. Like most other psychic abilities, this touch sense is very useful for diagnosing an energy or even a physical deficiency or malady. Teresa Brady shares this in her book: "Among many methods—from feeling hot spots or cold spots to feeling a disorganized energy flow in and around the body or particular organs—the medical intuitive can use clairtangency in addition to other methods to diagnose and treat disease." (Brady, 2011)

By utilizing your psychic sense of touch, you can learn many things about someone's particular ailment or weakness. Similar to clairsentience, by laying your hands on someone and using clairtangence you will be able to tune in to the flow of their energy system and determine if there are any missing or void areas. You can also tell if there are any deficiencies in their physical body, like muscle pain or tooth pain or even broken bones or past surgeries. Using clear touch can also tell you if there are any malfunctioning or missing organs.

I regularly see a client, Cheryl, who was having many issues with feeling like she was choking while doing exercises with her chakras. It would always be a problem around her communication chakra. She wasn't able to hear any messages clearly, nor was she able to put to words the information she received. I tuned in to her body by touching her hand. After telling her she was blocked in that area in some way and that it could be physical, she set out to discover what the blockage was.

Cheryl went to the doctor and, lo and behold, it turns out she has a thyroid disease. The thyroid is located in the throat and communication chakra area. Her block was a physical one. Now she needs to work out energetically why this happened so she can clear her fifth chakra and hear the messages she knows she's receiving. By using the psychic sense of touch, we were able to make the physical discovery so she can now get help.

We often use clairtangency during my workshops. During one of them I had a student, Jackie, tell me she was going through some medical issues and wanted to know if anyone could diagnose what was going on because the doctors hadn't been able to tell. She was very worried there was something seriously wrong and was desperate for answers. So after I held her hand and tuned in, I decided to have the whole class touch her, one by one, and tap into her energy field.

"What are you picking up?" I asked the first student.

"I feel like there is something with her stomach," she replied.

"Okay, and what do you get?" I questioned as the next student came up.

"I'm not sure but I feel like there's some kind of distress in the digestive system also," he replied.

On and on it went, everyone tuning in to the digestive area and stomach.

"Is this accurate?" I asked Jackie.

"Yes. I went to the doctors, but they don't see anything," she responded.

"I think it's an allergy. I was picking up on some kind of irritable bowel as well, but I think it's caused by allergies. Have you ever been diagnosed with dairy allergies?" I inquired.

"No, but it does seem to bother me after I've had cheese or ice cream. I have milk in my coffee every day, too. I wonder if that's what it is," Jackie responded.

"There's a visualization exercise I do whenever I have any kind of digestive distress. Imagine a press, like a big block of cement pushing gently down through your entire abdomen, leaving no room for anything to get left behind and cause pain. Try that. It may help to get everything out that's causing you distress. And I would use nondairy creamer and lay off the other dairy products for a couple of weeks and see how you do. Let us know!"

Jackie did just that. She cut out the dairy. She told me she was pain free. No more digestive or bowel issues. Our psychic senses had helped her ease her physical distress. Jackie is able to live a healthier, more comfortable life without worrying there was something more critical wrong with her.

Exercise: What's Wrong

Now that you've become accustomed to touch, get together with a few friends and invoke your circle of protection around everyone.

Then, lie down with your socks and shoes off. (Make sure your feet are clean!) Have each person take a turn and hold your feet. After they've done this for five to ten minutes, have them write down everything they get using their clairsentience. But don't share until everyone else has had a turn. After all of your friends have had a chance, compare what they've written. Did any of them hit on anything that is going on either physically or energetically with you? How about emotionally or mentally? Did they pick up the same things? Did they tune in to different things? Were they accurate?

After you are done in the hot seat, so to speak, switch. Have someone else be the sitter. Each person takes a turn tuning in by holding on to the feet of the person in the chair. Once again, compare what you've written down. Did you all pick up similar issues with your clairtangence? Or did your answers differ? Were you able to tap into any medical, physical, energetic, mental, or emotional problems?

How did you do specifically? How did it feel to use your clairtangence in this way? Did you feel all right when people were reading you? Or did you feel uncomfortable? Did it feel better to be the reader or the sitter?

Touch on This

Believing you are like Mr. Miyagi from the movie *The Karate Kid* can be a little hard to swallow. Knowing you are able to lay your hands on someone and diagnose an illness, disease, or problem is pretty intense, not to mention riddled with responsibilities that most people will not even attempt to take on. But allowing that you have the gift of clairtangence, and that this ability is a natural and normal part of you, can prove you're worthy of more than you know.

Receiving messages through touch can open a new chapter in your life and make you more aware of the power of your psychic abilities in a whole new way. Through touch you can understand. Remember, though, that even though you are excited about reaching out and touching someone, they may not want you touching them!

Telepathy & Psychokinesis

"The human mind will not be confined to any limits."
—JOHANN VON GOETHE

Telepathy and psychokinesis are not part of the clairs, but they are psychic abilities. Basically, telepathy is mental communications or communicating through the mind without using words. Psychokinesis is essentially the movement of an object or objects using only your mind without physically touching it. These psychic gifts are more common than you might think.

Do You Hear What I Hear?

Telepathic activity works in a few different ways. One way is to implant a thought, a word, or an idea into someone else's mind, either intentionally or unintentionally. Another is to have a mental conversation with someone else, no verbal communication necessary. Mentally causing someone to do something is also a form of telepathy. And finally, a little psychic spying—listening in to someone else's thoughts, probably without them being aware.

"What did you say?" I asked my husband.

"I didn't say anything," he replied.

"Yes, you did. I heard you. You said you were hungry," I charged.

"No. Actually, I didn't say a word. I was just thinking it. You read my mind," he answered, not shocked at all.

We have a connection, not surprisingly, as we've been together for a couple of decades. This is very common for people who know each other well. You've probably heard of people who finish each other's sentences or regularly say the same thing at the same time. This is not coincidental; it is telepathy. We may not always realize it, but it's there, this telepathic ability, under the surface, waiting to jump up and show itself. It is a regular occurrence between my husband and me.

These telepathic communications, hearing or knowing what someone else is thinking before they say it aloud, can be awesome. The other way this conversation plays out is that I take on what my husband was thinking; and again, this happens a lot.

"Hmmm. I'm hungry," I tell Tom.

"Really?" he responds. "I was just about to say that."

"Then you must have sent it to me telepathically because I wasn't even hungry a minute ago. I don't know where else that could've come from," I answer him, knowing full well that I picked the thought straight out of his mind.

Believe it or not, it just happened. Right this very minute, after I just wrote the last couple of paragraphs. We are sitting in the living room and I'm writing. Tom is watching a show on television. All of a sudden, I had a desire to try the apple caramel bread we bought yesterday from the local orchard where my daughter works.

"So," I asked him, "how is the loaf cake?"

"Oh my God. Why don't you write a chapter on that? I was just debating whether I should have a piece of that or a piece of the apple crisp," he chuckled.

"Wow. I *am* writing a chapter on that!" We laughed.

I wasn't hungry, but he implanted the thought because he was thinking it.

"This is not a good way to diet," I tell him as we move into the kitchen together to get a piece of the apple caramel loaf.

Exercise: Do You Hear Me?

Your friends are your best sounding boards. Have someone sit with you who is willing to play in your psychic world. Before you begin practicing your telepathy, it's time to clear your mind. And above all, protect it from any negativity.

Get into a comfortable position—it's time to relax. Take a deep breath to calm your mind. Breathe three more times, inhaling deeply, and as you do imagine that you are blowing a huge soap bubble all around you. It is transparent but rainbow colored, protecting you from anything that may pierce it with anything but positivity. Then, expand that bubble to include your partner. This will help shield the two of you from allowing anything else to penetrate the sphere of protection, keeping your thoughts pure.

Then, sit across from each other. Get ready to start practicing using your telepathic abilities. Have your partner think of an animal. Don't have them do anything else besides think about it. What is it called? What does it look like? What does it sound like? What color is it? Have them focus on the animal species, not the animal's name (for example, a Welsh corgi instead of a dog named Sadie).

Concentrate. Try and tune in to what your partner is thinking. Usually, but not always, it will be the first thing that comes to your mind. When you question it and second-guess it, you can lose it rather than hone in on what your friend is thinking of.

When you think you have the answer, tell your partner. Were you right? Were you wrong? Were you close? How did it feel? Did it feel comfortable? Were you sure you connected telepathically only to find out you were off? Or, were you sure you didn't connect but it turned out you were on target?

Try it again. Have your partner think of a color. Again, do the same thing. Were you right? Wrong? Was it easier to do colors versus animals? Were you close? Was the color on the opposite end of the color spectrum?

Try it once again, this time using numbers. Have your partner pick a number between one and one hundred. Have them envision it on a number line,

see the number, say it over and over again in ⱦ
head. Then tell them what you think the num
is. Were you in line with what they were thinkɪɴɢ:
Totally off? Were you in the right ten? (For example, the number was twenty-three and you guessed
twenty-seven.) Did it feel good? Bad? Did the numbers feel more comfortable than the animal and the
color? Or did it feel off?

After you're all done, switch. Have your partner
tune in to what you are thinking. Did you do better
this way? Are you a better sender than receiver? Or
did it work better the other way?

Phone Telepathy

So, maybe your cell phone doesn't sound like the old home
phones anymore, but regardless of the ringtone, the telephone plays a big part in telepathy. When you think about
someone, you send that thought out into the universe. This
creates a telepathic connection between the two of you. It
doesn't matter how much distance there is or where you are
located, the telepathic waves have been transmitted and are
there for you to pick up on.

Think about how often the telephone rings. Twice a
day, five times a day, twenty times a day? Out of those calls,
are you able to intuit who the caller is for any of them? Do
you reach to pick up the phone and call someone only to
find that they have just dialed your number and it rings in
your hand? This happens to me countless times over the
course of a week.

When the caller holds the telephone in their hand, they send energy into the atmosphere. This can create a link to the receiver of the call. Why does this happen? Because our thoughts, our brainwaves, are carried like wireless transmissions through the ether and can be directed to where they need to go. Imagine something as simple as a wireless remote control. There are no physical attachments, but the transmission and receipt of that transmission are present. Telepathy works much the same way; someone sends out the signal and someone catches it.

Similar to the actual phone call is the telepathic message you send for someone else to actually call you. This can be done on purpose or accidentally. Have you ever thought of someone and then seemingly out of the blue they call you? Or you think of them and then sit down and open your e-mail account and lo and behold there's a message from them? This, in particular, has become more prevalent in my life.

"I'm sure this is no surprise to you, but I'd like to make an appointment for another session," Nadine wrote in an e-mail to me.

She was right. This was not a shocker. The reason I was not totally blindsided by her e-mail was because I had been looking through my files the previous day and her file just stood out to me for no apparent reason. I was looking for someone else's information, but hers jumped out. This made me wonder why it seemed to elevate itself over all the others. So I focused on it for a minute or so and then moved on to what I was doing. This is why, even though it should've been, it wasn't a surprise that Nadine contacted me the next day. It was very cool.

"I'm not that surprised, but I am happy you are coming in again!" I responded to Nadine. I went on to explain why I think it happened.

I sent out the vibe. I was the one thinking of her. She picked up on my energetic phone call and reached out to me. Although this form of telepathy is customary in my life, I am still impressed and awed when it happens—even if it only happens with friends rather than clients. If I think of them hard enough, for whatever reason, they'll text me.

Exercise: Call Me!

This exercise is going to be fun! You are going to mentally reach out to some friends and see if they call you back. Make a list of people you want to contact you. Don't write down more than five people. After each person's name, record what you know about that person. It can be who they are, what they do, what your relationship was, or a fun memory of time you've shared. Focus on what you've written down. And then, just let it be.

Move on to the next name on the list. Once again, record anything you want about that person. Imagine them texting you or calling you or even e-mailing you. Imagine running into them at the store or on the football field. Concentrate on what they look like and the last conversation you had.

Finish going down the list and writing everything you want about each person. Once you are done, focus on each name and think about what they will say the next time they get in touch with you. Then, all that's left to do is wait.

Do they reach out to you soon? Within the hour? Does it take longer? A day? Maybe two? How do they contact you? Who does it first? Is it your closest friend? The one you expected to connect to you soonest? Or were you surprised by who heard your telepathic call first? Did they all respond to your mental message?

Tell each one what you did. How do they react? Were they surprised or had they been thinking of you? Was it a shock to them that you sent out your wireless communication? Or did they know it already?

Try this with other people as well. Are there certain people you can do it with more than once? Have some fun with it.

Just Keep Swinging

Many years ago I remember hearing about a high-level official from another country going on national television stating he was being invaded. He claimed the US government had implanted thoughts and ideas into his mind and it was using telepathy to sway his own thoughts and ideas. This was quickly glossed over in the media and never mentioned again, but the possibility that it happened definitely has merit.

Imagine a whole group of people sending the same message directly toward someone. Think of the impact that could have. The previous exercise had you singularly reaching out with your mental brainwaves to make someone contact you. How much force would it have if you had multiple people concentrating as one? We have the ability to truly change someone else's mind.

I discovered my own telepathic power during a workshop. In this class I was a student. The teacher, Margaret, a wonderful person, was discussing telepathy and the idea that we can use it to influence people. I didn't necessarily believe this was possible. Not that I didn't think we could exercise power over someone else, I just wasn't so sure we could truly infiltrate another person's thoughts. As she was leading the class, I began to think about what was going on in her mind.

All of a sudden she stopped mid-sentence and turned to me. She gave me the strangest look—a mix of surprise and almost fear. I didn't quite understand, yet, what exactly was occurring, but I knew she felt me.

Margaret continued running the class. She was lecturing and answering questions from the other students. As I sat there, listening, I was tuning in to her mind again. I was trying to prove or disprove whether telepathy actually worked, though I wasn't specifically setting out to do this. I was just casually thinking about it; however, I was directing my thoughts toward Margaret.

Again, she turned and looked to me. This time, the frustration was no longer masked.

"Would you please get out of my head? You're making me very uncomfortable!" Margaret said aloud.

I was shocked and embarrassed. I hadn't meant to make her feel distressed. I didn't even really believe her the first time she had looked at me, questioning. The rest of the students all turned, bewildered; like me, they too were unsure. Nevertheless, now I was a believer. Now, I thought it was very cool. I had never intentionally done this before, this intense telepathic communication.

I apologized and explained that I hadn't realized it really was happening. We all laughed, albeit a bit uncomfortably, and then we continued listening to Margaret teach. She instructed us to think of something, anything, and try and send that to our partner. I ended up with a woman I'd never met before, which I was glad of, and we began the exercise.

She went first. I recall she was thinking of a cupcake. I don't remember what kind, but I remember we did pretty well. Then it was my turn. I had to think of something to send her. We had been instructed to visualize it every possible way, feel it, and imagine it was really there. So, that's what I did. I sent it to her as strongly as I could.

When Margaret asked if anyone wanted to share, my partner raised her hand.

"How did you two do?" she asked.

We hadn't gone over what she thought I was sending her so I, along with the class, was anxious to hear what she had to say.

"I'm not really sure what Melanie was thinking. All I know is I feel really dizzy. I feel like I was going back and forth, back and forth, like a swing. It was actually a bit intense and was making me nauseated," she answered Margaret.

"Does this make sense?" the teacher asked me.

"Perfect sense!" I replied, shocked.

"I still feel a little sick to my stomach. I feel like wind was blowing the front of me, then the back, as I was swinging back and forth, and it felt like I was almost flying," my partner interrupted.

"Well? How'd she do, Melanie?" our instructor inquired.

"She did awesomely! I was sending her a swing. At first, I just envisioned it. I pictured it in my mind and saw the color, the texture, what it was made out of. Then, I began imagining I was swinging on it, and that it was getting really big. So big, in fact, that it began to feel as though I was flying!"

I was excited now. She got it! I was still shocked but incredibly energized by the whole thing. The only problem was, my partner was not. She looked at me as if I was from another planet. She didn't get how cool the whole experience was. I think that day was one of the first times I truly understood that although I am a very down-to-earth, normal, average person, I was different. Margaret just smiled at me knowingly. She understood. She then taught the rest of the class how to protect themselves from unwanted telepathic experiences.

Exercise: Swingin'

Your friends are your greatest asset when it comes to practicing telepathy—after all, it's not as though you can just walk up to a random stranger and ask if you can read their mind! So, again, for this exercise grab a friend or friends and ask them to get together with you for some psychic fun.

As usual, protect yourself. You want to allow each other into your sacred space, but you don't want anything other than positivity to come in.

For the first part of the exercise, have all of your friends close their eyes and breathe deeply. Instruct them to open their minds to whatever message or object you are going to send them. You are going to send them a swing, as I did in my class.

The reason you are going to use a swing is easy—you can see it as a tangible item, but you can also feel the movement along with it. Have your friends try and tune in to what you're sending them for at least three or four minutes. You want to really get the swing moving back and forth in your mind and project that energy out to them.

When you are ready, have them open their eyes and give them pens and paper. Tell them to write without speaking, what object they thought you were sending. Tell them to list everything it made them feel and all that they saw, heard, tasted, or smelled.

When they've recorded everything, have them put their pens down. Then, have each of them, one by one, tell you what message it is they received from you. Did anyone get it right? Were they close? Were they all off? Did any, like my partner, feel nauseated or dizzy? How did they react to having you infiltrate their minds? Did it bother them? Did they like it? Were they, like me, of the opinion that it was cool?

Afterward, have them all decide on one object to send to you. When they're ready, close your eyes and allow your friends, as a group, to telepathically send you the link to their object. When you are ready, open your eyes and start explaining what you received. Were you right on? Were you off? Did it feel good? Did it feel bad? Did it feel natural? Did it feel uncomfortable? Was it chaotic? Were you seeing it, feeling it, hearing it, tasting it, etc.?

Have your friends, if they want, take turns each sending you something on their own. Are you able to tune in to the object they're sending? Was it easier than the group object? Harder? Were you way off? Did it feel better or worse?

Keep playing, but make sure that you close the circle afterward by protecting yourselves individually. You don't want people leaving themselves wide open to anyone else telepathically projecting something into their minds!

Psychokinesis

Psychokinesis, also known as PK, is the manipulation of an object by using only your mind. Telekinesis is an older term, which means the movement of an actual physical object, again using only your mind. Sometimes the two terms are used interchangeably or as one generalized term, which I also will do. This seemingly superpower is used a lot less frequently than the clair senses.

Many people have heard of Uri Geller and the amazing feats he has accomplished beyond spoon bending. "Uri Geller is one of the world's most investigated and celebrated mystifiers." (Urigeller.com) He is known for his abilities to manipulate and move objects using only his mind. He realized at five years old that he had this gift when the spoon he was eating with curled up and broke in his hand. This happened without applying any physical pressure but merely using psychokinesis. His résumé includes working for and with the government, domestic and foreign dignitaries, and multimillion-dollar corporations. He is a pioneer in psychokinesis and telepathy. But this gift is not limited simply to famed mentalists. Though not a simple accomplishment, it is also accessible to everyday, average people. Like telepathy, we need only to practice to acquire it.

Psychokinesis is the ability used to bend spoons and roll pencils across a table without using anything but mind over matter. Those are just examples, but it is this thought energy that moves the objects. There have been many scientific studies done to prove or disprove psychokinetic ability. Most notable was J. B. Rhine's study, which was met with skepticism as it didn't prove beyond a shadow of a doubt that telepathy and psychokinesis were real. This didn't stop people from proving it to themselves, however, and there have been many people working on bending their own spoons.

There have been a multitude of books and movies involving psychokinesis. One noteworthy one was Stephen King's book *Carrie*. A remake of the book's movie has recently been produced, bringing psychokinesis back into the spotlight. In the movie, the main character, Carrie, who has been repeatedly alienated, made fun of, and ridiculed by her classmates, uses her telekinetic powers to teach them all a lesson. Though she uses this ability for revenge, it is this demonstration of the power of psychokinesis that stands out in the movie. Carrie's command of this gift is highly exaggerated, but it is based on the basic premise that thought waves can be sent out into the universe to influence and manipulate items. Learning how to do this takes time and practice, but it can be done.

Exercise: Move It!

Are you ready to try moving something? We are going to start off with a simple object because it is light and airy. For this exercise, you'll need a feather.

Once you've gotten your feather, clean a section of your table. Make sure that there are no spots on the table and lay your feather down. Then, sit and relax.

Close your eyes and take a few deep breaths. Imagine your toes are digging into the earth with roots coming out of the soles of your feet. Feel these roots as they travel down, all the way into the middle of Earth. Allow these roots to connect to a boulder at the axis of the planet, securing you, centering you, and grounding your energy.

Feel the earth's energy as it travels up through the roots into your feet and up into your ankles, shins, and calves. Allow that beautiful earth energy to continue, traveling up through your knees, your thighs, and into your hips. Let it move farther up into your reproductive area, your abdomen, your solar plexus, and your chest. Feel the energy as it moves up, continually clearing any negativity and debris. Allow the energy to move up through your chest and into your neck. Continue that energy flow up through your chin and your cheeks, through your eyes and your forehead, all the way out the top of your head. Any debris or negativity just falls away from your body back down to the earth to be recycled into positive energy.

Take another deep breath. Now, you are ready. Open your eyes and focus on the feather that is sitting on the table in front of you. Imagine the energy you've just enhanced reaching all around you toward the feather. See that energy stretching out, pulsing gently, pushing the feather away from you. Focus intently on the feather as the energy of your thought moves the feather even more, farther from you. You may feel a tingling sensation as your feather moves as if still connected to wings.

When you are done, you can pull your energy back so as not to expend it and exhaust yourself. Did you move the feather? How did you feel? Did you see it move? Did it move less than an inch? Did it move more than an inch? Did it move a foot? Did you just notice the fluffy down moving and not the entire feather? Or did you move the entire plume with the energy of your thoughts? Was it easy? Did it take a lot of effort to use your psychokinesis?

If your feather didn't move on your first try, that's okay. Do not give up. You can try again now or you can try again later. Don't be discouraged if it didn't work immediately. Most often you will find it takes many times to accomplish even the smallest of movements. Enjoy the process and focus on the feather. Eventually you will cause it to shift. You may even make so much progress that the feather ends up off the table.

Bend This

If you are looking for proof, don't necessarily look to the outside world. Look to yourself. "Scientists and scholars will debate the existence of psychokinesis for many decades into the future," says Jeffrey Mishlove, who claims space intelligence gave him his psychokinetic powers. (Mishlove, 2000) Whether you believe in extraterrestrials or not isn't the debate; the question instead is really, "Can I do this?"

Spoon bending seems to be a very silly thing to do, but for a long time it has been a benchmark used to measure psychokinetic abilities. Metal objects tend to hold energy better, so it actually makes perfect sense to use this as kind of jumping-off point. The act of the energetic force that causes the spoon to bend is the gift; the outcome of the spoon is just a byproduct. When you think about the processes of the brain and how little we actually utilize this most incredible organ, the concept of bending a spoon with psychokinesis becomes more of a possibility.

There was a children's television show called *Avatar: The Last Airbender*. It was about different tribes of people, some nomadic, who shared a common theme. Each tribe had a telekinetic ability. One tribe was able to move water, one fire, and then there was the last airbender who, you guessed it, moved air. The concept that entire tribes can have psychokinetic abilities is not too far-fetched when you think about the genealogy of psychic abilities. For example, grandmothers pass down their psychic knowledge to their children who pass it down to their children, all of which are naturally gifted to begin with. Families that don't have that in their bloodlines tend not to know much about psychic senses or psychokinesis.

Exercise: The Not-So-Last Spoon Benders

You guessed it—you're going to need a spoon. For your first attempt, I would try and stay away from sterling silver spoons. You don't want to ruin them! Just as you did with the feather, clean a spot on the table and place your spoon there, face up. Now, get comfortable. It's time for a nice, long meditation.

Before you begin, close your eyes and breathe deeply for at least one minute. As you inhale, you are breathing in energy to create reserves necessary to move mountains. As you exhale, you breathe out any doubt and negativity you may be holding on to that no longer suits you.

Now imagine columns of energy streaming out of the bottoms of your feet, going through the earth and spreading out under the ground. Imagine it spreading like a pond under you, creating a buzz all around you and through you. As this energy pool extends, it also rises through your legs and your torso, right up through your neck and shoulders, and out the top of your head. Feel the tingling sensation as it pours like a beautiful silver waterfall all around you. Imagine this silver energy bending and swaying as you move your hands, your arms, your legs, and even your neck and head. See this silver waterfall projecting out, controlled by your own thoughts, two feet out, then three feet, then ten feet. Feel it moving like liquid mercury wherever your mind directs it.

Keep your eyes closed and do nothing else except play right now. Make that silver puddle move all over, creating shapes that extend farther and farther out. See, in your mind, the curves you create and the shadows caused by the energy. Imagine making fingers that reach out and push away from you. Once you've envisioned this mercurial energy as it morphs into different shapes of your own design, you are ready.

Imagine those mercurial fingers reaching out toward the spoon you've placed on the table. Now these fingers are special—they are like an iron fist and are full of unparalleled strength. Push these fingers out farther and wrap them around the entire spoon. Feel the energy of the mercurial hand as it begins to squeeze the spoon, bending the handle. As your energy, this mercurial hand continues to squeeze, getting stronger and bigger, so much so that it radiates excess energy making the spoon begin to glow. As the spoon glows, imagine it is heating up from all of your energy. As it heats up, your mercurylike fingers grow even larger, squeezing even stronger, bending the spoon even more.

Now the hand has grown so big it separates, dividing into two hands that are holding the bent spoon between them. You are able to push your energetic hands together, pressing as hard as you can, bending and stretching the spoon even more. Keep going until you are exhausted from manipulating the energy around you.

When you're absolutely spent, breathe deeply and pull your energy back in, recharging yourself as the mercurial fingers suck back into the silver waterfall around your body. Then, breathe again, deeply, and feel yourself taking the energy back in, drawing from the reserves to revitalize and renew your body, mind, and spirit. Take another deep breath and open your eyes.

Look at your spoon. How does it look? Did it move at all? Did you bend it? Does it look exactly the same? Don't be discouraged if it didn't change—after all, this is your first experience with spoon bending! Pick it up and feel it. Does it feel hot? Warm? Cold? Room temperature? How did the exercise feel overall? Did you believe it could work? Did you think you would fail? Are you going to try it again? How do you feel now? Tired? Exhilarated? Excited? Frustrated? Happy? Sad?

Above all else, feel great about yourself and what you just did. Regardless of the outcome, you attempted to move matter with only your mind! That's what superheroes do! You are an incredible and energetic being! Be happy!

Mind Over Matter

Telepathy is not just fun, it's also useful. During a job interview, it would be great to know exactly what the person hiring you is expecting you to say. Knowing when someone is telling you the truth or not is advantageous no matter what the circumstance. Sending someone the message that you love them and care about them even if they are on the other side of the world is priceless. Telepathic communication is indeed valuable.

Psychokinesis definitely has its merits as well. On the extreme end of the spectrum, imagine being in the position to move a beam that's fallen on someone or even lift up a car to rescue someone who's trapped and being able to do it. Think of the practical benefits as well; reaching the pen you need by rolling it from the other side of the table or turning off the light you forgot to switch off when you got in bed so you don't have to freeze your toes off getting up.

You have exposed the myth and done so much work that your brain must be abuzz with overflowing energy. You've taken what most only whisper about and attempted to make it your own. This is incredible in and of itself. You've tried to communicate, telepathically, with your friends, and tried to move an object and manipulate another using psychokinesis. You are amazing! Give your brain a break and relax for a bit. You've proven the possibility exists for telepathy and psychokinetic powers to be a normal part of your life. You deserve to put your superpowers on hold and rest.

Combining the Senses

"There can be little doubt that we possess
an insatiable curiosity about the future."

—SCOTT CUNNINGHAM

Psychic senses rarely are autonomous. Simply stated, they frequently work together, in tandem, to provide you with psychic insight. Seldom does it happen where only one sense will be used, though you may have one that's more prevalent than another. For example, I may smell something sweet and then have an image of a birthday cake. That's my clairalience and clairvoyance working together, or one right after the other, to provide a better depiction of what I'm tuning in to.

Sometimes multiple images are necessary to cement the idea or the impression you receive. For instance, using the same example, smelling something sweet in and of itself could mean anything. But if you smell something sweet and then receive an image of birthday cake, it could indicate your sister who has passed is wishing you a happy birthday from the other side because your special day is coming up next week. This is a frequent occurrence during my sessions; it is very unusual that I will only employ one of my psychic senses. It is not something I do intentionally, but it is something I leave myself open to having happen.

This combination of clairs helped me bring comfort to someone recently in a session. Morgan came in for a reading and was hoping to connect to a deceased loved one. She obviously knew who she wanted to talk to, but I didn't. So, I had to use all my gifts to tune in, or rather, the person on the other side had to send me the information in such a way that I could use all of my psychic abilities.

After we were about half an hour into the session, I began smelling evergreen or pine trees, so I asked her if it meant anything to her.

"No, I don't recall anything. Well, maybe," she said, changing her mind.

"Oh, all right. What does it mean to you?" I queried.

"We have a few pine trees behind our house?" she responded, in question format.

Normally I let the client tell me what something means. After all, it's regarding their life, not mine, so who am I to judge what they associate it with? This time, however, that just didn't feel right.

"I don't know if that's what it is. Unless those pine trees are very significant in some way, I think it has to be more than that," I told her.

"Hmmm. They are just trees in our backyard. I don't think they are significant."

"All right. I'm seeing an old-fashioned adding machine now, the kind where you push down on the number and it stays down until you pull the lever back. Is someone an accountant? Does that mean something to you?"

"No. I don't know what that means," she answered, frowning.

"Well, now, I'm hearing the words, 'Every time a bell rings an angel gets *her* wings,' which is from the movie *It's a Wonderful Life*. Does *that* mean anything to you?"

"Nope. Sorry. I'm not understanding."

Every time I do a reading, I always tell my clients to not try too hard to make things fit. Sometimes it's difficult to not take that to the extreme.

"Let's look at this all again. The pine scent, the adding machine, and *It's a Wonderful Life*. This is definitely a reference to Christmastime, and someone who passed. It's either got to be that someone close to you died in December around Christmas or their birthday was in December. It's also got to be someone who did something with finances or accounting, because I'm seeing the adding machine. Finally, it's supposed to be 'Every time a bell rings an angel gets *his* wings.' I heard *her* wings. So this tells me it's a female. She's working really hard to get you to recognize her," I told Morgan.

All of a sudden it was as though a light bulb went on. I could see the wheels turning, and her eyes lit up. I knew she had figured it out. It was the person she was hoping to talk to—her sister.

"Wow! I'm sorry. I wasn't getting it! She died in December and worked at a bank!"

"No apologies necessary! I'm just glad it makes sense. She says to wish you a Merry Christmas this year. She doesn't want you to be sad. She wants you to be happy," I shared.

"That's awesome. Thank you so much," Morgan replied sincerely. She got what she wanted: her sister had come through. It took a little while to understand the clues, but there she was.

Exercise: Tuning In to a Combination of Abilities

Learning how to tune in to a combination of psychic senses is really not that difficult. After all, you're not limiting the way you receive the information by only psychically listening or seeing. For this exercise, you will allow all of your psychic senses to be wide open to receive.

Breathe deeply while calling upon your circle of protection. Then think about someone who's passed—someone you may have had a significant connection to. And sit back and relax. Allow all thoughts, images, sounds, smells, etc., to come. Be open to any impressions you receive. Sit with yourself fully accepting for at least five minutes, longer if you're up to it to give yourself time to communicate.

Afterward, write down everything that came through, whether you believed it to be a true message or you felt it was your imagination. Did the messages make sense? Did you receive visions? Symbols? Words? Scents? Other types of impressions? Which psychic abilities do you think you received information through? Was it the first time you ever got communications using any of the psychic senses that helped you today? Did you like the process? Did it bother you? Were you comfortable or uncomfortable? Would you do it again? Did you feel you didn't receive anything? Did it make you happy?

Helping Another to Live On

Cindy came in to see me. She and her family were devastated by the loss of her sister. She had been brutally beaten to death by her boyfriend, who, rather than live the rest of his natural life with what he'd done, committed suicide immediately afterward. I picked up on all of this during her session. Her sister, Michelle, sent evidence to let Cindy know it was really her. In order to tune in to the evidence, she sent it to me in a number of ways.

I knew something had changed at Cindy's work because my claircognizance was kicking in.

"Maybe, I'm always making changes," she told me.

"No, something is different," I replied.

Now I was seeing an image with my clairvoyance of something to do with fashion—a hat or a hairnet or something on her head.

"Did you get a new hairnet or something? Do you wear one for work? Because I can hear Michelle laughing about it!" I chuckled, having heard her with my clairaudience.

"Yes! Oh my God, she would laugh about that!"

"That's not all she's laughing about. I'm feeling kind of giddy about the Broncos beating the Giants. So, either she was a Broncos fan and you're a Giants fan or my clairsentience got something wrong," I continued.

"Wow! That's exactly right!"

We were batting a thousand. Her sister Michelle was coming through loud and clear. Giving me messages utilizing all of my psychic abilities was allowing me to share the communications more completely with Cindy.

"Aw. Did someone have a baby? She's talking about a name and I'm seeing the cuteness. She told me she's honored," I kept going, still using a variety of senses.

"Yes, our cousin named her new baby after her. They gave her Michelle as a middle name. That makes me happy that she knows they honored her in that way," she smiled.

So far Michelle had come through with flying colors. She was able to share so many things with Cindy that there was no possible way she wouldn't be acknowledged. By communicating with me through all of my psychic senses, I was able to give her a more comprehensive reading. Most of the messages were just minutiae, little details that really didn't mean much, but they absolutely signified so much. They were the evidence Cindy needed to confirm her sister's presence. What I received next, however, was incredible.

I kept hearing "red rocks," which made me think of when I went out to Sedona, Arizona.

"Is there an Arizona connection?" I asked Cindy.

"Umm, no. She lived in Colorado before, though. That's kind of close?" she responded.

"I don't know. I'm seeing stones or rocks." And I started drawing a stone wall.

What happened next was kind of strange. I became acutely aware of my lungs, as they expanded and contracted, breathing in and out. I could feel the breath and how it was sending life through my body. So I shared this with her—and she cried.

"Is there another *M* name? I'm picking up that she's with him?" I wasn't sure what this meant, but I felt all of it together was very significant.

"Wow. Michelle had marked 'organ donor' on her license. Mark, a stonemason who lives in Arizona, received her lungs because he needed a transplant. She *is* always with him."

It was my turn to be honored. The goose bumps were flying up and down my body. I was awed by the magnitude of what I had just received. Michelle was an incredible spirit; even in death she lived on to save another soul. I was blessed to have been able to share this little bit of her.

Exercise: What Do You Get?

Take inventory of yourself. Understanding what would connect you to people you know may help you understand what connects other people to their friends and loved ones. What are some things that stand out about you? If you needed to make yourself known, without actually being there, what would you do? Would you try and make someone hear something about you? What would that be? Would you show them something? What would you show them? Would you make them feel something about you? What would it be? Would you have them just know something? What would that be?

What details about you or your life would stand out enough so that people would know they were tuning in to you?

Amnesia?

Psychic amnesia is a term coined to describe when a psychic or intuitive channels information that a client or partner cannot readily identify or acknowledge. This does not happen because the information you are receiving from your guides, angels, or deceased loved ones is inaccurate. Rather, it occurs because the person getting the reading is so focused on one or two particular items or connecting to a certain dead person that they have psychic blinders on and don't recognize anything else in the moment.

One way to distinguish if you or the person you're reading is suffering from psychic amnesia is to notice whether or not you keep receiving the same impressions. Repetitive messages, even when they come through various psychic senses, generally point to a communication that's not being identified.

This exact thing happened during a gallery event I was holding. It was a good night; a lot of messages were coming through and being delivered to the right people, until the little animals showed up. Yup, that's right—the little animals.

"I'm picking something up about little animals. I keep hearing that I need to talk about the little animals. I think

I'm over here, on this side of the room," I stated out loud to the audience of well over 125 people.

The chatter began: "What kind of little animals does she mean?" I heard whispered.

"I'm talking about teeny little animals, though I'm not quite sure what it's about," I continued.

This time I had a few people in the general vicinity of where I was looking stake a claim to the little animals.

"Well, growing up we had mice? A lot of mice," one person said, hopeful that it was for her.

"I think it's more significant than that," I responded.

"We had guinea pigs," someone else shouted out. "They were little ones, not big."

"Sorry, don't think that's it."

Everyone comes to these events with the wish they will be read. We all want to hear from our loved ones on the other side. Naturally, people want to believe what the medium is picking up is for them.

"But they were really quite small for guinea pigs. People used to ask me why they were so small. That's significant, isn't it?" they challenged, hoping.

"I don't think that's what it is," I asserted. "Sorry!"

As is often the case, the real little-animal person was not claiming them. So, figuring they'd lost their chance, I moved on.

"I'm still over here in this area. I am picking up something about clowns now. I suppose it could be me. I mean, my last name is Barnum and my father was actually in the circus. I've got clowns coming out my—!"

"Achoo!" someone sneezed.

I laughed. We all laughed. Perfect timing.

Again, no one was really claiming the clowns, but not for lack of trying.

"I don't like clowns. Could that be it?" someone said.

"I had a stuffed animal clown growing up?" stated another person.

"Ah, well. I'm pretty sure I'm right up here, now," I said, pointing to the front row. "I'm picking up a male figure. He's showing me cancer."

Finally, Tory, who was connected to the male, acknowledged it was for her.

"I think that's me," she said.

"Was this your father? I'm feeling like he was in construction or was a builder," I continued.

"Yes it is, and yes he was."

"I'm hearing he had his own business but that he also worked for someone else. He was a helper or a volunteer or something," I said.

"Yup, he had his own business and he worked in the hospital. He always volunteered for things his whole life," the woman answered.

"Great. He's making me feel like the cancer was pinpointed in one area but that very quickly it had spread throughout his body," I told her.

"You're right," she said, a bit teary.

"And does the letter *W* mean anything?"

"Absolutely does. His name was Warren."

"Wow, okay. I'm getting the little animals and clowns again. Do you know what this is?"

"Nope. No idea."

"Well, maybe I just need to move forward. Now I'm getting ice cream? Please tell me you know what that's about!" I asked her.

"Sorry, but no," she answered, kind of embarrassed for me.

"Really? I'm seeing ice cream cones?"

By now, I'm a bit embarrassed for myself. What the heck is happening? Why am I getting all of this gibberish? It doesn't make any sense.

"Oh," Tory exclaimed suddenly, "I think that's for my cousin Cathy!"

"Great! Is she here?" I asked feeling like maybe we were finally getting somewhere.

"Yes, I'm right here!" I heard and looked to my right, at the front of the room.

It was my event promoter, Cathy. I think she was more shocked than I was.

"We are opening an ice cream place, my husband and I!" Cathy said enthusiastically.

"I'm hearing it's going to take a bit more time than you're expecting—just be ready for it!" I told her.

"Okay, thanks! Oh wait … oh my God. Don't kill me! The little animals and the clowns are for me and Tory, my cousin, the one you just read for," she exclaimed.

"Do you two carry them in your back pockets?" I joked.

"No, but her dad was my uncle. Both of our parents had little animals on a display shelf. They were these tiny little animals, just like you were showing us when you kept asking—little animals. My mom collected owls and also clowns, and she displayed them on a shelf in the living room. Her mom," she pointed to Tory, "my aunt, collected skunks!"

"Wow. And who's the *M* name connected to the ice cream shop?"

"I don't know," Cathy answered.

"I'm hearing it again so it has to be significant," I told her.

"I don't … oh, wait. That's my husband! Mike! Wow, I so was not expecting this!" she said, laughing because she had just been hit with psychic amnesia.

Tory and Cathy didn't recognize what I was talking about because they weren't expecting messages to come through in that way. I used all of my psychic senses to try and make the communication as clear as possible. Their case of psychic amnesia just made it necessary for me to utilize everything I had for clarity.

Exercise: Remembering

Boosting your memory on a regular basis will help you to avoid psychic amnesia. It will also be an asset when trying to recognize or identify symbolic or oblique messages when they come through using your psychic senses.

Get a deck of cards, preferably something other than regular playing cards. If you can use tarot cards or angel cards or the like, it will be better for the purposes of this exercise. Shuffle the cards and then deal out ten into a pile. Put the rest of the deck off to the side; you won't need them for a while.

Take the ten cards and turn them over, one at a time, looking at them as you do. Once you've flipped every card over, go back to the first and flip it again so you are looking at the back of the card. Continue until all of the cards are turned backside up.

Now, pick up a pen and paper and write down every detail you remember from each card, beginning with the first. Do you remember what each was? If you don't remember a specific card, tune in to your clairs and see what they tell you. Write it down, making a note next to that entry so when you go back you'll know it wasn't your memory, but a psychic impression that had you recording your impressions of that particular card.

When you are all done, flip the cards over again and compare. How did you do? Did you remember a lot of details? Did your psychic senses come in clearly? What methodology was prevalent? Were you able to accurately write down each card? Can you describe the colors and the pictures on the cards? Is there a title or number for each card that you've remembered?

After you've compared all of the information you've written down for each card, do it again. Shuffle the deck and deal out another ten cards. When you've completed the next round, match up what you've recorded versus what the actual cards were. Did you remember more this time? Did you need to call on your psychic senses to help you more or less? Were you accurate? Did you get more information right on this second attempt? Or less? How did it feel? Did it make you nervous or uncomfortable? Was it natural?

Do it again, but this time shuffle only the last ten cards and reuse them in a different order. Once you've finished recording everything, compare how well you did this time around versus the other times. Was it easier because the cards were more familiar? Or did it not make a difference?

Review all of your data. Do you feel your memory has been bolstered? Do you feel tired or energized? When you are all done, drink a lot of water. That will help you to refresh and cleanse any energy that was drained by tapping into your temporal lobes, the part of your brain that controls your memory function.

Multiple Senses for One Party

When I do private parties, I get really nervous. No matter how long I've been doing this work, I still worry that no one will show up—no one that's dead, that is! I do gallery-event-style gatherings, meaning a dozen or more people will get together and I deliver messages to those in the audience. Worrying, even in this type of small venue, is what happens just about every time before I begin.

Getting up and speaking in front of the guests is not what concerns me; that I have no problem with. It's what's out of my control that I worry about, the loved ones that need to visit and come through. So, in order to better my chances with the powers that be, I employ all of my psychic abilities rather than trying to tune in with just one.

Yesterday, I did an event for a wonderful group of women. There were a lot of what we affectionately called "dead peeps" coming through from the other side. Using the full spectrum of psychic senses, I was able to channel loving and even healing messages for everyone. As a matter of fact, so much information came through when I opened up all of my senses that the session that was supposed to last one and a half hours ended up running almost three hours long! After much laughter and tears, we all agreed the dead peeps had come through for us; they did their thing and helped me share their messages through the utilization of all of my psychic abilities.

Take Care of Yourself

Psychic abilities are powerful. They can also be overwhelming on occasion if you are tired or if you are tuning in for a long time. This is another instance when it's so important to be open to all of the intuitive gifts. When you allow the information to come through from the other side in whatever way is smoother or more natural, it's easier and less work for you. By not blocking anything out, except of course negativity, it creates a more seamless opening for channeling, making it less taxing and, of course, more effortless to connect to the other side.

When you work for a long duration with your psychic gifts, whether it's for other people or clients or for yourself, you can drain your energy. If this happens, it can cause negative physical manifestations such as headaches, nausea, or even sore muscles. It's important to ground yourself to revitalize your energy.

You've been practicing using so many of your psychic senses. You've done an incredible job tuning in and protecting yourself, but there is always room for more grounding. Feeling sick is a huge deterrent when it comes to wanting to utilize your intuition. After all, if something hurts you in some way it would be silly to continue beating yourself up, right? So, many people will stop practicing or step away from their psychic senses because they don't know how to renew their mind, body, and spirit. Luckily for you, there is a simple way.

Exercise: Ground Yourself

Now's your chance to recharge! One of the simplest ways to do that is to go outside. Find a patch of grass or dirt and take your shoes off. Dig your toes in and relax. Just stay there, in this space, and breathe. Let any exhausted or negative energy drain into the earth, leaving you with only positive energy. Being at one with the earth is the easiest way to reboot your spiritual system, which in turn will invigorate your physical system as well.

Or find a tree. I don't care where you have to go to do this; just find one. Once you've found it, it's time to hug it. That's right, just hug it. Connecting to the earth in this way helps release any negativity while absorbing positivity.

Nope, That's Not for Me

This exhaustion hit me recently while I was doing a private party. I had been doing individual readings for twelve people in a row, fifteen to twenty minutes at a pop. Tapping into everyone's energy, one right after the other, was definitely tiring. It was about ten p.m. and I still had about an hour and a half to go, four more people from what I understood.

When I do readings, even if it's just quick fifteen-minute sessions, I try and take a couple minutes between and write down whatever information I tune in to. Because I was exhausted, I didn't try to use any particular sense, I just opened my instincts wide and listed what I got. That's why, during the next reading, I wasn't 100 percent sure what I was intuiting was on point.

"Hello! Have you ever had a reading before?" I asked my next client, Gina.

"No, this is my first," she answered, somewhat hesitantly.

"Okay, great! So you're a reading virgin!" I exclaimed.

Usually, this gets a laugh out of people, breaking the ice and relaxing them. With Gina I got nothing, not even a slight upturn of the mouth. I decided it was going to be a long fifteen minutes.

"So, the first thing I wrote down is that you work diligently. I feel like you are not ecstatic about your current place in life, but everything is pretty much going okay. There's nothing seriously wrong in any way," I told her.

"That's correct. I don't really know why I'm here. I told Martha I didn't believe in this, but she said to come anyway," she confided.

This was great. Not only was I exhausted, but I had to prove to her I was for real.

"Well, let's hope you have a good experience, then!"

I continued with the reading; there was nothing too exciting. Then I got down to the end of my paper. I had drawn an image.

"Does Christmastime mean anything? I'm seeing the image of a tree. Maybe it has to do with trees?"

"No. I don't know what that means," Gina responded, deadpan.

"Okay. I'm also feeling someone digging in the dirt? It may not physically be you but it has to do with you?" I continued.

"No. Again, I think you're off."

"Hmm. All right, well it has been a long night!"

I tried to loosen the atmosphere by chuckling. Her expression didn't change. She just looked at me, waiting.

"What about horses? Does this mean something to you?" I tried.

"I don't really know what you're talking about. This is not about me," she insisted. She was sure there was no way I could connect to her energy.

"Well, I saw trees, I feel like digging in the dirt, like a farm, and I'm hearing horses whinny," I continued.

This time I was a little frustrated. Sometimes I'm off, but this time it felt like I was dead on.

"Are you sure this doesn't have anything to do with you? Do you work on a farm? Maybe a tree farm?"

"Well, yes, I work at a tree farm, but I don't dig in the dirt or ride the horses. I don't take care of the trees. I do accounting inside," she told me, serious as could be.

Really? None of it made sense to her? I was beginning to understand her skepticism. Some people just need everything to be perfectly spelled out in order to trust that it is for them. Gina was one of them. It didn't matter how many impressions I shared with her. She couldn't justify it—it seemed beyond logic to her. But I knew. I was dead on. I was tuned in to her energy. It was okay that she didn't believe it. I was good with that. She thanked me, I thanked her, and we called it a night.

Gina's reading took all of my psychic senses to perform, and even then it wasn't easily validated. Every now and then that happens. We are all doubtful about things we don't understand. I'm even skeptical at times. I don't always accept everything as true, either.

Exercise: Skeptical?

Grab your pen and paper. It's time to use your memory again. Write down any instances you can remember when you've had doubt about your or someone else's psychic gifts or their ability to tune in. Not just a generalized intuition, but any specific occurrences.

After you've written down all you can remember, it's time to revisit them. Do you still feel the same way? Do you think it was because of the person? Or did you doubt the validity of the psychic senses? Do you feel differently toward the person or psychic abilities now?

If so, why? If not, how come? When was the last time you felt skeptical? Are you still skeptical?

Superpowers!

Elaborate divination systems have been in place since the beginning of time. Your own intuitive gifts need not be any less elaborate. Think of all of the superheroes. There's Superman, Spider-Man, Wonder Woman, Thor, Green Lantern, and many more. They all have a unique or a *super* power that makes them special. You have intuition. You are no less special than they are! And you are a real, living human, not a cartoon fantasy.

Your five physical senses can be supersized or enhanced through the use of your psychic senses. Think about what you can see with your physical eyes. Imagine if your sight could be improved using your clairvoyance. Or what if your hearing could be augmented through your clairaudience? The implications of joining the two separate, yet connected senses are vast, not to mention awesome. You may already be employing this in your daily life without even realizing it.

I have a difficult time driving at night. It's even worse during bad weather. When it's raining and dark, I cannot see. It's even harder when there is a car coming toward me with its headlights on. I feel temporarily blinded by the bright beams. I have glasses, but even then there are times when I really just can't see, and obviously you need to see to drive!

On one particularly bad night, I was driving in a snow-storm. I was doing okay until it really started coming down.

The area I was driving in was pitch black; there were no street-lights. The only illumination was my car's headlights. Every once in a while I would come head to head with another driver and, again, I was blinded. It got to the point that I was going to have to pull over in the middle of nowhere. The problem was the storm wasn't supposed to be ending anytime soon, and I couldn't just sit with my car off because it was way too cold.

So, I did the only thing I could think of to do. I pulled over and I asked my guides, angels, and deceased loved ones to allow my psychic sight to enhance my physical sight. Immediately after that, I felt goose bumps. I started driving again, and within minutes I had a car coming toward me. I got nervous, worried that I would be blinded, but almost as if in a time warp I saw everything clearly—the oncoming car, the snow, the road, the painted lines on the road. I was not blinded. Thankfully, my sight was enhanced by my clairvoyance.

Choosing to combine my psychic senses, as well as the critical issue that I actually had to see where I was going, seemed reason enough for the universe to help me out. I was fine during the rest of the drive home. Supersizing your psychic senses is a great thing; supersizing is only a problem with fast food!

Exercise: Supersize It!

Think of a physical sense that you'd like to enhance. Your hearing? Your eyesight? Your sense of feeling? Improving your physical senses will also help your psychic senses.

For this exercise we are going to focus on your eyesight. Pick a tree with leaves or something that has a lot of detail and stare at it. Focus on the details of it and then call in your clairvoyance to help you see it even clearer. It may seem the colors become brighter or more intense. It might seem like everything gets larger. Stay with this, focusing in for at least fifteen minutes.

Supposing it was a tree, did it change the way you saw the tree? Did it get brighter? Darker? More detailed? Larger? Smaller? Did it seem deeper? More three-dimensional? More flat or one-dimensional? Did you feel too close to it? Too far from it?

Try it again with a different object. Did it work better? Worse? Was it clearer? More detailed? Less detailed? Easier? Harder?

After you are all done, practice supersizing your other senses as well!

You Are a Superhero!

Combining all of your psychic senses and using them together or in tandem makes your intuition more accessible and more accurate. Letting go of all of the self-imposed restrictions regarding which psychic ability to use gives you the capacity to open up to the other side greater than ever before. Don't worry about the process or how it works; just expect that you will utilize all of your gifts, just like a super-hero. You have a boundless capacity to connect to all of your psychic senses.

eleven

Psychic Tools

"We shall not fail or falter; we shall not weaken or tire…
Give us the tools and we will finish the job."
—SIR WINSTON CHURCHILL

We use a variety of tools in our daily lives to make it easy to accomplish tasks. Knives and pans make it easier to prepare meals. Computers make it easier to write. Hammers make it easier to build things. Cars make it easier to travel. The list goes on and on. Tools have been around since the dawn of time. From rocks to airplanes, every tool we have serves a purpose—to make something in our lives easier.

Psychics also employ the use of tools. Divination tools run the gamut from tea leaves to crystal wands and just about everything in between. Tools don't make someone psychic; they simply assist that person with tuning in to their own intuition. While professional psychics devote their lives to developing their intuition, the reality is anyone can become skilled at using divination tools without having any previously recognized psychic ability. With practice they will successfully be able to read someone, though usually not as well as someone who is fluent with their psychic gifts. There are a number of different tools available to help with just that purpose.

The divination system works by using our own personal energy waves. We send these waves out into our possible future, allowing that changes may occur to adjust those current patterns. I believe the tools are a means to translate those invisible energy waves that are streaming through the universe.

Oracle Cards

Cards are probably the most prevalent form of divination tool out there. There are all types of oracle cards, including angel cards, tarot cards, playing cards, fairy cards, spirit cards, rune cards, and even mermaid cards to name a few. They are used to help guide you through the present, make known the past, and reveal any upcoming challenges or opportunities. They also provide guidance on successfully navigating the transitions.

Even with so many different types of oracle decks available, learning to interpret them by using the same basic guidelines makes them analogous. In order to interpret their meanings, one needs to look at and break down the design elements: colors, landscape, shapes, buildings or structures, people, angels, animals or beasts, words, letters, numbers, and objects.

There are two basic parts to reading the cards. Depending upon your preference you can look to the overall card first and then break it down by analyzing each part or vice versa. Taking in the whole picture and determining how it makes you feel is vital to understanding its meaning. Looking at what's displayed can indicate the intent of the card and whether it implies a positive or a negative vibe. After you've taken in the illustration as a whole, it's time to explore each element and the influence the elements have on each other.

The following are some generalized meanings to assist you in reading the cards and the various ingredients of each card. Remember, these are very basic generalizations. To fully comprehend the meanings, you need to do your own research and studying.

Color meanings:

- *Black:* negativity, wrongdoings, or a void
- *Blue:* communication, wisdom, cleansing, fifth chakra, clairaudience
- *Brown:* nature, groundedness, back to basics, down to earth, low energy
- *Green:* healing or need for, financial success, nature, fourth chakra
- *Indigo:* meditation or need to, philosophy, psychic, dream state, sixth chakra, clairvoyance
- *Orange:* creativity, sexuality, sensuality, reproductive system, physical move, second chakra
- *Pink:* female energy, healthy or happy, innocence, optimism, pregnancy

- **Purple:** (also violet) regal, power, strength, high honor, psychic ability, spiritual, enlightened, divine guidance, kindness, crown or seventh chakra
- **Silver:** divine communication, spiritual message, psychic, universal connection
- **White:** purity, divinity, intuition, angelic, truth, cleanliness, virginity
- **Yellow:** happy, power, cheerful, intuition, clairsentience, third chakra

Number meanings:

- **One:** the beginning, basic, root
- **Two:** partnership, duality, balance, manifestation
- **Three:** creation, fertilization, elemental expression, amalgamation
- **Four:** structure, foundation, security, stability
- **Five:** struggle, conflict, disruption, discomfort, loss
- **Six:** rebuilding harmony, communication, success
- **Seven:** good and bad, victory and upset, perfection and inadequacy
- **Eight:** progression, movement, mastery, acknowledgement
- **Nine:** nearing completion, struggle, fulfillment, compromise
- **Ten:** cycle completed, review time, transition, ending

Object meanings (also note condition of object, i.e., run down, shiny and new, etc.):

- *Greenery:* nurturing, healing, growth
- *Flowers or fruit:* growth, spirituality, happiness
- *Cup or bowl:* mission or challenge, position in life, Holy Grail, emotions
- *Structure:* physical body, our façade, protection, stability
- *Angels:* divinity, help, trust, faith, guidance
- *People:* presence, profession, another person who influences situation

Different decks will display different drawings and designs, but the artwork provides the overall feeling of the card. Having an artistic slant can add to your ability to read them. Such was the case when I was at my sister's house. Everyone wanted me to read for them using tarot cards, but I suggested they try and read the cards for each other. Having had no real previous exposure, my stepniece, Lauren, jumped right in and began.

"Just tell me what you get, in any way. Don't judge it or censor it," I told her.

"Okay, here we go!" Lauren said.

She looked at the pictures on the cards and began spinning a tale of what it meant, specifically for me since she was reading me. As usual, I don't remember the details, but I remember thinking how impressed I was with how good she was at it. Lauren is an artist. She regularly taps into her artistic and creative side. She read the cards using that angle, and she was right on.

Exercise: In the Cards

For this exercise you can use any card deck you have access to. Angel cards, tarot cards, and even regular playing cards will work. However, the more detail on the card, the more details you'll be able to pick up for your reading.

Invoke your protection and then take a few deep breaths. Shuffle the deck, and when you feel you have energized the cards enough deal out three in a row. The first represents your past, generally over the last six to twelve months. The second represents your current state, or place in your life. And the third represents your possible future.

Look at each card, beginning with the one all the way to the left, your past. Look at the overall picture. Does it make you feel good? Bad? Sad? Confused? Happy? Scared? Excited? Then take each individual aspect of the picture. What do you get from them? Colors? Objects? Numbers? Does this make sense as far as your past goes? Does it coincide with your time over the last year or so?

Do this for all three cards. Write down everything you pick up on for all of them. Does it feel good? Does it make sense? Do you feel you are biased in reading them because it's for you? Did it feel easy? Hard? Were you able to read the cards without too much of a struggle?

If you want, do a reading for a friend. Make sure you tell them you are new at this and they should take their reading with a grain of salt! Let them try and read for you as well. When you're all done, give each other feedback. How did you do? How did they do?

Remember, practicing and learning the meanings for the cards will help you to excel, but trusting your instincts is just as important. Don't give up if it didn't feel right immediately. Practice makes perfect! Or, as close as you can get to perfect when reading oracle cards!

Rock On

Rocks and crystals carry energy and are used sometimes as tools in the psychic world. They are available in all different shapes and sizes, and each kind has their own properties. For example, one of my favorite crystals is rose quartz. Rose quartz is helpful if you're feeling lonely. It can represent love, friendship, and peace. It is also useful for emotional healing. Amethyst is also a crystal I like to have around. Corrine Kenner, an expert with crystals and rocks, describes amethyst as " … widely used by psychics, who find that amethysts' soothing energy gives their intuitive senses a boost." (Kenner, 2006)

These crystals and rocks hold energy and can be used as a gateway into your own intuition. By holding one in your hand, or touching one if it's very large, it can be used as an instrument to connect you to your psychic senses. It's almost as though you have a magic wand, and in fact, some crystals are shaped in the form of wands. Crystals have been touted to possess a kind of magical power, and they are potent. In order to harness their power, you need only to hold them.

I teach a workshop called Expanding Your Awareness. In this class, one of the exercises I have the students do is pick a crystal or a rock that speaks to them. I have a number of different stones, and each person is encouraged to choose the one that feels the best to them. I like amethyst and am regularly drawn to it. So, I think most people will be. But I am always amazed by the stones that some people choose—especially the ones that are very basic.

Crystals and rocks have their own natural shapes, designs, and inclusions. When you start looking at them, you'll notice different patterns or even faces forming. During one session, I began to see a whole scene play out in a large piece of quartz crystal.

"Okay, Jill, I'm getting a colder atmosphere, so I think the time frame is winter," I said.

Jill was in my workshop, and I was demonstrating how to read the crystals. She asked me when I saw her getting a job that she would actually enjoy. What I saw when I looked into the crystal was a park with trees and a path and everything was covered with snow.

She then asked, "Do you see me alone at that time or with a significant other?"

I looked into the crystal again and the images that I saw changed. I was now looking at the backs of two people holding hands in silhouette, but what was interesting was both had long hair. Were they friends? Or were they lovers? I wasn't sure whether it was two girls or her and a man, so I told her as much.

"Well, I see you with someone around the same time. But I can't tell if it's a friend or significant other. You both have long hair and it's a woman?"

"Ha! That's because I'm gay!" she replied, laughing. "I wasn't sure whether you'd pick that up or not!"

"Well, there's your answer. Yes, you will be romantically involved with someone in the winter!"

Jill was trying to trick me, but the crystals were not lying. Holding the quartz, I could feel the energy reverberating. I saw many different pictures in the crystal that were giving me answers. By holding a rock or a crystal, you can let it begin to tell you a story based on all the different pictures you see in it. You also may feel or know something as you handle the rock or crystal. So much information will be provided to you simply by touching it.

Exercise: You Rock!

In order to work on this exercise, you'll need to pick out a rock or a crystal. If you don't have one, and you're not able to buy one, just go outside and look for one that resonates with you.

Hold the rock in the palm of your hand and close your eyes. Take a deep breath and let yourself relax for at least five minutes. Feel the energy the rock is sharing with you. Does it bring anything to mind? Is it making you feel anything? Is it hot? Cold? Do you feel happy? Sad? Excited? Bored? Healthy? Sick? Does anything else come to mind? When you are done feeling the energy, it's time to open your eyes.

Look at the rock or crystal. At first, you may just notice the color or the shape. You might also notice any veins or inclusions. Keep gazing into the rock. Notice if it turns cloudy at all or brightens up. Do any shapes jump out at you? Do you see any words, letters, or numbers? Do you see any people, structures, or landscapes? Does the crystal seem to be changing shape or morphing into something other than what it was? Again, after looking at it for at least a full five minutes, think about what you saw in the rock. How did it make you feel? Did it make you happy? Sad? Excited? Did it feel comfortable? Uncomfortable? Good? Bad? Clear?

Try this with more than one type of rock or crystal. Compare whether it feels easier or better with one type over the other. Take note of how much information you get off each different category of rock or crystal.

Pendulums

Pendulums are another tool used by psychics and nonpsychics alike. Using a pendulum is known as dowsing. "The pendulum is deceptively simple. With just a few minutes of practice, anyone can use it," says Richard Webster, author of *Pendulum Magic for Beginners*. (Webster, 2002) Pendulums are simply a weighted item suspended on a piece of cording, string, thread, or chain that spins or rocks with your hand performing as a fulcrum. The simplest pendulums are made with wedding rings, sewing needles, or even paper clips used for the weight. More advanced and commercially made pendulums can be composed of crystal, wood, and even glass. As with crystals or rocks, pendulums can speak to you. You may choose one over another based on how it feels to you.

Pendulums can be used to answer yes or no questions, directional questions, and more. There really is no limit to what answers you can gain from a pendulum. Many people design pendulum cloths or sheets to place under the pendulum with prewritten answers. While holding the pendulum dead center over the cloth and asking a question, the pendulum will move toward the answer, without any help from the user. Adding letters and numbers will give you access to even more answers, as the letters can spell out names and words and the numbers can, well, give you a number!

Holding the string at the top, wrapped over your middle and index fingers with the weight at the bottom, is the best way to use a pendulum. This helps ensure you're not moving the pendulum yourself by accident. The energy that stirs the pendulum is coming from the universe through your subconscious, into the pendulum. You don't want to add your own movement. When I teach others how to use one, I always tell them to hold the pendulum over their other palm and request, "Show me yes." This allows you to see whether it will spin or go back and forth for an answer in the affirmative. Then I instruct them to request, "Show me no." It should provide them with the opposite of the yes. These two directional answers, yes and no, are the beginnings of dowsing.

Anyone who chooses to continue to use pendulums will end up with a favorite pendulum. Whether it's made of a crystal, a carved piece of wood, blown glass, or something homemade, it will be the one that you resonate with. I have a favorite—it is a lead fishing lure weight on a piece of string that was made by one of my teachers about twenty years ago. I used it in the class and was actually frightened by it. The amount of movement I had from the pendulum was insane. Everyone in the class was shocked, myself included.

"Show me there is energy flowing through," I said to the pendulum while the rest of the class asked the same of their divination tools.

My pendulum began swinging from left to right, immediately picking up speed and velocity to the point that it was horizontal. I dropped it, scared. There was way too much energy going through it.

"Wow. What is going on?" I asked.

I picked up my pendulum and felt an extreme heat coming off of it.

"Try again," everyone said.

So, I tried again. It was totally still, so I said, "Show me yes."

Once again, my new pendulum was so energized it went horizontal.

"Oh my gosh! What is happening?"

They told me not to worry, that this was great.

"I don't know if I like this. It's way too strong. I feel like there's too much energy going through it. It's kind of freaking me out!" I said.

This time I asked the pendulum to pare it down.

"Show me yes. Slow it down," I said.

The pendulum, which had started going horizontal immediately slowed down. It was now manageable. I didn't feel as though it was possessed this time. I was able to use it after that, and it's always been the most energetic responder of all my pendulums. Added to that one pendulum, I have a couple of rose quartz, a couple amethysts, a wooden, a crystal layer, and many more, but the fishing lure weight is still my favorite.

Pendulums have been around for a very long time. They've been used to find and locate water or oil, show which direction is the best for a new settlement to move the tribe to, and even determine whether a pregnant woman would have a boy or a girl. No matter if you are using a pendulum to decide what dress to buy, which football season tickets to invest in, whether you'll have a new relationship, or whether you should take the new job, it's an easy way to divine which route you should pursue.

Exercise: Swing It!

Get yourself a pendulum. Go to a new age store or bookstore or even a jewelry store and see which one speaks to you, which one feels right. If you don't want to buy one, that's okay. You can make one with string or thread and a ring or even a paper clip.

Then, make a list of yes or no questions you'd like answers to. You don't want to ask more than ten to start, but be sure to write them down so you won't need to think about them. You don't want your thoughts to interfere with the energy you are channeling through to the pendulum.

You're going to start out simple. Once you've got your pendulum in your hand, place the string around your middle and index finger, grasping with your thumb to hold it. By doing it this way you cut down on the natural movements your hand makes no matter how hard you try and hold it still.

Now, send energy into your hand by imagining a clear channel traveling from the top of your head through your neck and shoulder down into your hand. Place your other hand under the pendulum, creating an energy pocket. Say aloud, "Show me yes," and see what the pendulum does. It will either spin or go back and forth. Once you have a definitive answer, say, "Stop moving." Then, do it again asking this time, "Show me no," and wait for the response.

Once you've received your answers as to which is a yes and which is a no, it's time to start asking the questions you want answers to.

How does it feel? Does it work for you? Does it make sense? Did you get answers for everything? Did it feel like the pendulum was moving on its own accord? Or did it feel like you were moving it? Did any of the answers surprise you? Did you get the answers you expected?

After you've completed all of your questions, put your pendulum down. If you want to ask more, go ahead now and make another list. Then start from the beginning, asking for yes and no, etc.

Try using different pendulums, ones you make and some from the stores. Have fun with it!

Crystal Ball Gazing

Crystal balls have, to the unaware, been linked to gypsy fortunetellers and Halloween witches. This is fine because the basic premise of the crystal ball is to see something no one else can see. Anyone—whether a gypsy or a Halloween witch or a normal, average person—can learn to use this divination tool to access answers.

Like other divination tools, crystal balls can be used to forecast, or read, the future. Author Alexandra Chauran gives some important advice, "Before you get on a roll with practicing the flow of readings with your crystal ball, it is important to do some experimentation to find out how your own perception with the crystal ball is going to work. Each person's perceptions may vary greatly." (Chauran, 2011) Practicing can bring you to an understanding of just what it is you are seeing.

To read a crystal ball, you must first place it where it won't be shadowed. You want the ball to be as clear as possible so any images you see will be undiluted. In order to read using this tool, begin by focusing not on the actual shape of the ball, but instead focus on the inside area of the ball. Let yourself see any shapes that may start to form. The shapes can appear as clouded images or dark outlines. By forming questions in more of an open-ended "what would the benefits be?" or "what would be the outcome if…" way, you will receive a more accurate answer. Staying away from yes or no questions will provide you with better detail.

Many years ago, I was doing a reading for Brenda at a psychic fair and she was asking which home she should buy. I didn't know what the choices were, but I was ready to jump in. She noticed all of the various tools I had spread across my table and requested, half jokingly, if I would do her reading with my crystal ball. I obliged, though usually I used my small crystal ball as decoration as opposed to a divination tool.

"I don't know which house to buy," she said.

"Don't tell me anything else! I want to see what comes without knowing anything beforehand," I interrupted her.

She nodded and I began. I started looking into the crystal ball, gazing into the middle of it. I saw three columns of shadow spreading through it.

"Are you considering three different homes?" I questioned.

"Yes, we are," Brenda responded, surprised.

"Okay, let me see which one will be the best for you," I continued, my confidence bolstered a bit.

I looked into the crystal ball again. All of a sudden images started to form, almost as if someone painted them in with a light gray ink.

"I see what looks like sailboats and a dock. I'm also seeing windows, lots of windows," I told her. "Does that mean anything to you?"

"Wow. It means everything. One of the houses we are considering has a bank of windows overlooking Long Island Sound," she replied in awe. "That is my husband's favorite, but I was afraid of the water."

"Well, I think you will be happy there," I answered, seeing the sun in the crystal ball.

Exercise: Crystal Ball Gazing

While most people do not have crystal balls lying around their homes, some do. If you are one of the lucky ones, yay! If not, you can find one in a holistic or new age store or even a cheap version at a Halloween costume or a party store. If you still don't have one, use a glass vase or at the very least, a glass. Just make sure it is smooth, not crystal or cut glass or anything that would create shadow.

Now it's time to ask a question of the crystal ball. It's a simple question, but the answer can be extremely detailed. "What do I need to know about my future?"

Then, wait. Focus your eyes and your spirit entirely on the crystal ball. Look inside it. Notice if any shapes begin to form. They may just appear as cloudy or fuzzy shapes. Pay attention to any changes in color or the way the texture looks or even the temperature of the ball. Does it change the way you feel? Do you see anything? Does it appear shady or shadowed where it wasn't before? Is it clear? Write down anything you see so you may analyze it when you are all done.

Don't worry if you don't see anything at first. Give it at least ten minutes. If you still don't see anything, you can try a different crystal ball. Remember, what you see may be symbolic, so don't discount it. For example, I just looked to my glass and asked when my book would be done (published) and I saw a bat—the kind that flies, not the kind that hits balls. This made me think of Halloween, which makes perfect sense because my release is in autumn. Be open to anything you see without censoring it. You may be surprised by what you see!

Tools, Tools, Glorious Tools

There are many additional tools to be utilized. Nature provides us with tools available to everyone. Like crystal ball gazing, try cloud gazing. Looking for images within clouds can give you answers to questions. If it's evening rather than daytime, look to the stars for divinatory pictures. Candle flames are very telling. By asking a yes or no question, you can receive an answer. The flame will bend one way for yes and one way for no. Determine which way is yes and which way is no before asking the question. All of these methods can help you make choices in your day-to-day life. Or maybe more significant, can make statements about your future life.

Finally, the casting of lots has been significant in divination throughout many cultures and many lands. Using items such as bones, runes, coins, tea leaves, dice, and shells can help you interpret what you have to look forward to. Many of these lots work together with a cloth or a board that has been specially designed to answer questions or divine the future.

For example, making a cloth with sections delineating topics such as health, home, finances, love, relationship, children, etc., are useful to gain access to a variety of answers. Runes, which are stones with inscriptions engraved onto them, each meaning something different, can be cast onto the cloth. Looking at where the stones land on the cloth can foretell what is coming. For instance, if the rune marked with the fertility symbol lands in the children section, chances are it's relaying someone's having a baby soon or someone recently gave birth. If that fertility rune lands in finances, it might indicate a new financial project or new money coming in due to a birth of a new idea.

Using that same cloth, coins can be cast. Assign each different coin a subject such as movement, growth, harvest, joy, fertility, protection, strength, love, partnership, self, defense, etc. Throwing the coins onto the cloth will provide answers or an outlook toward the possible future.

Exercise: Do What You Want

It's time to choose for yourself! Pick one of the above divinatory tools and set everything up. For example, if it's going to be casting coins, make sure to assign each one a subject.

When you've decided which method you will use, give it your all. Did it feel right? Did it feel off? Did it answer any questions you may have had? Did you feel good? Bad? Happy? Was it difficult? Would you use that particular tool again? Did you try more than one tool? Which worked better for you? Did you have good results with all that you tried?

It's All Good

Using divination tools does not make you psychic. Nor do you need to be psychic to use divination tools. However, you can help your psychic senses by using these psychic tools. If you are tired, the tools can assist you and make reading for yourself or others easier. If, for example, you

272 • *Chapter Eleven*

are working your first psychic fair and you need to do five readings in a row, using cards may be the way to go. It will allow your psychic awareness to come through by interpreting the cards you've flipped over. Again, you don't need to be psychic to use these tools, but it is definitely an asset. You have everything you need to predict your future.

twelve

Summing It All Up

"At every single moment, we are given the opportunity to choose our future. What we do today will determine what we face next week, next month, or next year. It is at the moment of a particular occurrence that we are called upon to make a choice: Will I do it the way I've always done it, or will I do it a different way?"

—IYANLA VANZANT

Extrasensory perception is a gift we can all take advantage of. Not always fretting about the mechanics of how it works affords us the opportunity to enjoy the benefits. Most people who develop their intuition don't do so to become famous psychics. You're probably hoping to be able to tune in for yourself, to help with everyday questions, or to connect to someone on the other side. Either way, most everyone is fascinated by the psychic hits—the connections made. And some are baffled by the information that comes through.

One of the myths about using intuition is that it's always foolproof and completely accurate. This is not always the case. There are times when the intuitive hits you receive through any of your psychic senses prove to be without error, but other times the guidance we are receiving is not as clear or can be fuzzy, which may lead to inaccuracy. We may also read a situation that gives us what we think is a clear-cut answer but it turns out we were mistaken—as good as we are, sometimes we are just plain wrong.

Alternatively, it can be more than just missing the mark altogether. Often, the symbols or the specific messages that come through are unclear. Don't forget, trying to tune in to your psychic senses can be like trying to tune in to a radio station in another dimension. Sometimes the lines of communication can be crossed and the information that's received can be a bit convoluted.

I had just this happen to me during a reading with Caretta. Caretta had come in because her daughter had been to see me and she purchased a gift certificate for her mom. Caretta wasn't necessarily a believer, but she wasn't quite a skeptic either. She was open to the possibility that psychic ability was real. A bunch of things came through during the reading. Then, I started receiving strange messages.

"Is there a reason I'd be seeing the Grand Canyon or something?"

"Maybe," she replied. "Anything else?"

"I'm getting the initial *M* connected to it?"

"Keep going," she answered.

"Well, I'm hearing laughter and they're showing me a big boat on wheels? I don't really understand what that means. Do you?" I continued.

"Ha ha ha!" she laughed. "I can't believe it! Everyone laughed at us!"

"Oh, you need to let me in on the secret!" I told her.

"My sister, the *M* name, and I decided we wanted to travel to the Grand Canyon, out to New Mexico and Arizona. But we didn't want to fly. We decided we wanted to drive, and then we figured we would rent an RV. Everyone laughed at us because neither one of us could drive it! But we are doing it! It is our boat on wheels!" she laughed, the skepticism erased.

This is more common than one might realize. The idea that there are a multitude of messages coming through all at once coupled with the fact that our messengers from the other side will send us information however possible can really mix things up. The information we get from the other side quite often will be subtle. This makes it even more important to clear your mind before trying to tune in. Usually we are able to sort it out. If we are not getting the messages for ourselves, sometimes we need help interpreting from the person we are reading for.

Our psychic senses assist us in receiving communications from the other side, but it is up to us to develop our inherent gifts if we want to be more adept at understanding them. We all have one or two abilities that are more prevalent than others, but we are able to increase all of our psychic abilities through practice. Developing your own vocabulary is helpful to enlarging your psychic footprint;

it broadens your ability to interpret messages. This includes symbolic as well as verbal communications.

When we look to psychic abilities to help manage our everyday lives, we have to trust the information we receive. Simply stated, when we get a message we have to know it's real and not just our imagination. Or when we have a déjà vu moment, we need to believe it's not just our brain skipping a step and putting our activities straight into our memory instead of our processor.

Déjà Vu

Déjà vu is a sensation you get when you walk into a building or a room and you could swear you've been there before even though you never have. Or the feeling that you've already had the same exact conversation with someone that you just started having. It may feel almost as though you're in a dream state, but you're not. You are wide awake and experiencing something your mind is telling you you've already experienced. I often have those déjà vu moments, but there was one in particular that really freaked me out.

I was looking at homes with a local realtor friend. She told me we were going to love the next place because it had everything on my wish list. Jenna said we would have to renovate, but that it would be great when we were done. When we pulled up to it one thing was very clear to me—I had been there before.

"Have we already looked at this place?" I asked her.

"Nope, it just listed a couple of days ago," she replied.

"Really? I'm feeling like I've been here before. I have a wicked sense of déjà vu," I told her.

"Well, if you were it wasn't with me," she stated.

I looked around the property as we got out. She told me it was situated on about ten acres and there was a two-story barn and a 1,700-square-foot house. As we walked toward the barn, I told her exactly what we'd find inside. Downstairs, built into the side of a hill, would be a basement with a half dirt/half poured cement floor. To the left, I told her, there would be a shower stall and hanging above, off the ceiling joists, would be hooks. I told here there would be a few homemade, crude tables lining the walls as well.

"Come on, you're pulling my leg," she said.

"No, really. I swear I feel like I've been here before."

Sure enough, the room was exactly as I described it, filled with dust and dirt and eerie feelings as well. The energy was stagnant, almost as though it hadn't changed in at least a decade.

"This is where they slaughtered the animals they hunted," I told her, looking at the tables. "And that old farm sink is where they washed their tools."

I was feeling nauseated.

"Oh my. How did you know? How could you know?" Jenna questioned.

She believed in psychic abilities. In fact, she had asked me for my psychic opinion about things before, but neither one of us was expecting this.

"Do you think you are just having precognitive flashes? Like, are you just seeing the future before it happens?" she asked me.

That would explain why I knew where everything was, but it wouldn't clarify how I felt. I truly believed I had been there before, and it felt almost as if I was in a time warp.

I didn't think that's what it was. I actually felt like the clothes I was wearing had changed into a long, cotton dress with an apron and it felt like early 1900s.

I shared this with Jenna and she said, "Okay. Let's try this. We will go inside, but before we do, explain what it will look like."

"There will be a staircase to the left, curving up to the right near the top. There are four small bedrooms off of a hall and one bathroom that may or may not have been renovated, but I remember there is a large heating duct with a brass filigree-like plate centered on the hallway floor. I'm not sure if it's the return vent or where it blows out, but it's big. The kitchen was yellow, but I don't know what it will be now. And there will be a living room, an open dining room, and another small room on the main floor."

We walked in the front door. The staircase was off to the left and you could tell it curved around. Every hair on my body was sticking straight out. I felt, not as though I'd lived there, but that I'd visited there. And I didn't like it. Sure enough, all of the rest of the information I had stated was evidenced in plain sight. Everything I said was staring us in the face.

"I have to get out of here," I told Jenna and ran out the back door.

I knew the house was old, and I could feel the energy there. There were older people who died in the home, whose kids had long since moved out. I didn't like being inside and found little reprieve being outside.

"Are you okay?" Jenna asked me, concern written all over her face.

"Yes. I'm fine. I just don't want to be here anymore," I told her.

My belief is that I had, indeed, visited this property before, probably in a past life. And I was sure I was also having psychic flashes that I almost certainly had the first time I had been there. I didn't like the energy. It wasn't that anything bad happened; I just couldn't take all of the death. The hunter was not a bad person; he just did a lot of killing to feed his family. I could feel the spirits of all of the animals in the barn. It was overwhelming. I wanted out, and we left.

Déjà vu is a powerful force. At times, it may be difficult to determine exactly what it is you're experiencing when you get that feeling. Sometimes it truly is a malfunction of the brain; the moment you're in goes straight to the part of your brain responsible for memory before it goes to the part that processes what you're doing. Other times it's more of a precognitive flash, a psychic foretelling of the future. And still, other times, it is a moment in time, captured, from a past life that you are reliving. There is one more possible explanation—we are part of multi-dimensional living, and are experiencing things over and over again. (I'm not so sure about that last one!)

Whatever you choose to believe, déjà vu is a normal occurrence and most people will have at least one episode during their lives. Next time it happens to you, embrace it!

Don't run from it or be scared by it. Learn as much as you can from it—you never know what it could do for you.

Exercise: Déjà Vu?

Get out that pen and paper. Think back to a time when you felt like you'd already done what you were doing. Search your memory for that feeling of déjà vu. Then write it down.

Where were you? Whom were you with? Had you ever been there before that you remember? Did it strike you as odd? Did you enjoy the sensation? Did you not like it? Was it detailed? Did you tell anyone about it? Did you question what it was or did you know it was déjà vu?

Was there another time you experienced déjà vu? If so, write it down! List every time you can recall that you've had the feeling you'd been there or done that before. Then, compare the experiences. Are there any similarities? Were the experiences in the same place or with the same person? Or was it different every time? Was it meaningful at all? Did you learn anything from the experience?

Being Present

Having a déjà vu experience can make you feel as though you're not present or in the moment because you are stuck between what's currently happening and what occurred previously. As long as you hold on to where you are and what you're doing, you are still acting and responding in the present.

When we rely too much on knowing what the future holds, we don't allow ourselves to live fully in the moment, and therefore we can't experience what we need to in order to learn and even possibly change the future. When I read for someone, I receive information about the probable future, but that future is not written in stone; it can change based on actions and decisions made in the present. If we don't live our lives now, how can we then exist and be present to make those adjustments or changes?

Being present also affords us the opportunity to, for lack of a better way to say it, earn brownie points or good karma. Not that we should simply act or do things in order to store up positive energy chips to be cashed in later; we should do good deeds or good acts because it is right and just. Helping others creates positive karma, which hopefully indicates we will have positivity coming into our lives down the road.

Karma

Karma is a Hindu or Buddhist idea that what we do comes back to us tenfold. In the Western world, we've also adopted this opinion, though we usually tie it to something negative. In other words, if we are kind or perform a kind act we will be gifted with a kindness in return at some time in our future. The same goes for negativity. If we are mean or do harm to someone, we will be retaliated against, either in this lifetime or the next. Karma is not based on a punishment or reward system, however. It is just an idea that the energy we put out is the energy we attract. Doe Zantamata states, "Good karma increases people's connectedness and collective good. Bad karma isolates people and results in a more self-centered collective." (Zantamata, 2012)

We can look at karma as being a reciprocal sort of energy sent out into the universe that works much like a boomerang. When we help someone in a situation, we may be provided with that same type of help down the road, or when we set out to deliberately or willfully cause destruction or mayhem to someone, we can expect that that also will be placed in our path at some point in our life.

Sometimes karma strikes sooner rather than later. This was evident with Kirk, a hunter who set out in the wee hours of the morning to try and "bag one." He had a deal in place with a landowner who had 100-plus acres on which he allowed Kirk to hunt for deer if he only used a bow. So, that's what he was intending to do early on that fall day.

He drove there, in his brand-new truck, and hiked into the woods until he got to his hunting blind, the perch he had created up in the trees to wait for his prey. He climbed up and settled in at six a.m. About five hours later, he was still no closer to taking home a deer, so he collected his spent arrows, packed up, and headed out.

He had missed two deer that morning; after each shot they seemed to have stopped, turned, and looked at him, almost, he thought, laughing at him. He felt as though they were taunting him, teasing him to show who was boss. As he hiked back through the woods, he had the distinct feeling they were watching him, eager to see him leave. He could feel they were angry.

He got back in his shiny red truck; no need to tie anything down in the bed, as he hadn't been successful at killing any animals. He took off his camouflage, hung up his bow, and started the engine. The ride out of the woods was uneventful. It was the ride back down the road, through the ridge, where karma struck.

The road was nestled between two hills, like God had pushed down a ribbon of blacktop, forcing ridges to rise up into woods on both sides of the street. As he drove down this road, out of the woods on the right came a deer. He didn't hit the deer. Rather, the deer jumped off the ridge and ran straight over the hood of his new truck and onto the other ridge, only to get swallowed up by the woods.

"Son of a—," he began.

He didn't have time to finish because in that moment as he watched the first deer disappear, there was a rustling off to his right again and a whole herd of deer charged out of the woods and followed suit—running right over the hood of his truck. He claims, though I don't know how true it is, that the last one, out of about ten, turned his head back to look at him. Kirk swears he saw the edges of the deer's mouth curl up.

Karma struck him a swift blow. He had gone there to hunt and kill those animals. Instead, they spared him and only damaged his new truck.

Karma, both good and bad, is sometimes recognized as this reciprocal energy and sometimes not, but it's there, always. It can help you help yourself, or it can allow you to hinder your spiritual and mental progress. It's your choice.

Exercise: Life's a Bitch, or Is It Just Karma?

Have you ever felt like you did something not so nice and then something just like it happened to you? Or if you are like me, you judged someone for how they acted or what they did and then found yourself in the same predicament? Karma can be swift. That, among other reasons, is why you should always strive to do good and be a better person. You should send loving vibes out into the world, not just because of karma, but because it's the right thing to do.

When was the last time someone did something wrong or bad either to you or to someone you love that had you saying, "Karma's a bitch"? Do you know of any other times? Did it make you feel better? Worse? No different? Did you want something bad to happen to them? Did you just move past it?

Today, go out and do one good deed for someone. Don't do it only because you expect to be paid back through positive karma—do it because it's good. Share a smile with someone, tip your barista at the local coffee shop, let someone out ahead of you in traffic. How does it feel? Did it feel right? Do you feel good? You've just changed someone's day. Your small act of kindness has created a pay-it-forward vibe and now, like the butterfly effect, you've begun something wonderful. Why stop there? Do something else! Feels even better the second time around!

Energy

The positive energy you've sent out into the world will ultimately affect you as well. Whether karma comes back around or not, we are all connected to the universal energy and can feel how it shifts and changes. It is this energy that we tap into when using our psychic senses and this energy that spreads love or hate.

Psychic energy has been tapped into since the beginning of time, since before there were skeptics who tried to prove it scientifically. The psychic senses used to tune in to this energy have given us a glimpse into a world we would otherwise never know, the possibility that there is more to life than what we are currently living. These powers, or I should say these superpowers, are available to all who wish to develop them on some level. To some extent, we are all intuitive. We are all rational, intelligent human beings born into this world with the desire to understand what it is and where we are. We have been given the key to interpret just that; we need only begin by opening the door, and opening our awareness.

Think back to the beginning of the book. In your mind, go over all of the exercises you've done and think about how far you've come in such a short time. You are incredible! Your spirit is unique and wonderful and ready to work for you! It's time to take advantage of everything life and the afterlife have to offer. You've discovered things about yourself that you never knew existed or that have lain dormant for years. You've learned how your mind, body, and spirit act with clairvoyance, clairaudience, clairsentience, claircognizance, clairgustance, clairalience, and clairtangence. You've discovered if you're talented in telepathy or psychokinesis and if these are abilities you are willing to practice. (Your friends may want to steer clear if you've discovered you are really good at telepathy!) And you've learned how your energy and your actions affect others in the grand scheme of things.

You have done more to discover who you are in a short time than many do in an entire lifetime! Enjoy your discoveries and repeat the exercises over and over to discover even more! You are incredible!

Past Lives

"All we have to do is remember: remember who we are and what we are, what we have been through, where we have come from, why we are here."

—BRIAN WEISS

Okay, really. Did you think we could talk about being born knowing without talking about past lives? Come on!

I am a Certified Past Life Regression Facilitator. What this means is: (a) I believe we've lived before; (b) I believe our past lives have everything to do with our current situations in life; (c) I believe we will do it all over again in our next lifetime; and (d) I have learned to help you all discover who you were before you were you!

We have been here before, this place called Earth. We've traveled, probably with the same pod of people: family, friends, and yes, even enemies. We've discovered things about ourselves that have helped us in those lifetimes as well as future lifetimes. We have been given the opportunity to learn and understand more fully the reasons we've done things we've done and how the universe works.

With every incarnation we are given the chance to redo things we may have done wrong. We are blessed with the opportunity to get it right this time so we may move on to learn other things. And we do this with people that also have lessons to learn. We can go back in time and space and discover things about ourselves we may not have known that have contributed to who we are in this lifetime. We can also cure fears and phobias we've carried throughout lifetimes. We evolve. And with every evolution, we come closer to living in pure love and to believing in the universal energy that is real rather than just blindly following any religion that is manmade in search of this love.

Past life regression is the process through which we are able to view who we were before. Sometimes this can be a fun experience and sometimes it can be traumatic, but either way it is what it is!

I had a client, Grace, come in many years ago desiring a regression session. She was not a believer, but figured she'd give it a try. She grew up Italian-Catholic, but she was kind of a hippie. She was a perfect candidate!

She sat back in the comfy, cozy chair in my office and we began. I was able to bring her into a past life quickly. Please note, I do not ever, at any time, influence who someone was in a past life. It is their experience and theirs alone.

Many details came out during the session, including locations in London, England, where she had lived in one of her past lives. She described perfectly a church, an orphanage, and a cemetery. She talked about the name of the street, the town, and even a plaque that was hung near the entrance. All of this with me asking generic questions such as "Where are you now?" and "What are you doing?"

When I took her out of hypnosis, she was filled with doubt.

"Was that real? It felt like I made everything up!"

I gave her a copy of all of the notes I took and she left, still unsure. About twenty minutes went by, and I received a phone call from her.

"Oh my God! I just looked everything up on the Internet! That church isn't even there anymore, but it was! And the name, the orphanage, the cemetery, the iron gate, and even the plaque were all there! There was a picture! It was exactly what I saw! Oh my God! I'm freaking out!"

I just smiled and told her she was awesome.

Past life regression can help you to discover who you are and can also uncover your psychic senses. It can assist you in opening up to your true spiritual self and allow you access to places such as the Akashic Records, a storehouse in the ether where everything everyone has ever done in every lifetime is recorded. It will show you your gifts and talents and even what is waiting for you to tap into and utilize.

The past life exercise to follow is intended for you to open up and discover your psychic abilities, but you can also use it for so much more! Enjoy!

Exercise: What Did I Know Then That I Can Reknow Now?

Get comfortable and close your eyes. Relax and breathe deep. Count down slowly from twenty down to one. By the time you reach the number one or even sooner, you will find you are relaxed, so relaxed in fact that you won't even have to open your eyes anymore. Go ahead and begin counting.

Good. You are relaxed now. Deep down. Imagine being in front of an old wooden bridge shrouded in fog. On the other side of that bridge is the entrance to a world in a time and space that has everything to do with who you are today, a place that has everything to do with what psychic senses you are empowered with.

When I count from three down to one, you will pass over that bridge to the place that has everything to do with who you are today. Here we go; three, two, one. Plant your feet firmly on the ground now.

Are you alone or with others? Is it dark or light? Are you inside or outside? What are you wearing? Are you male or female? If someone were to say your name, what would they call you? Where are you? Can you see any signs indicating where you are? Imagine you can see a calendar. What is the date?

Now, imagine there is a seat, either on soft grass or earth or a manmade seat, but let it be comfortable. Sit down. In front of you is a list of psychic senses. You have rocks. If you possess a natural inclination toward the psychic sense, you will place a rock to the left of where it is written. If you have not yet developed a psychic sense, place a rock on the right side. You will do this one at a time using the following list:

Clairvoyance

Clairaudience

Clairsentience

Claircognizance

Clairgustance

Clairalience

Clairtangence

Place the rocks either on the left for a sense you've already begun developing or that you're proficient with or on the right if it's one you need to start working with.

When you are all done, say the following words: "In this lifetime and all lifetimes I am an intuitive being. I am ready, willing, and excited to begin, from this moment on, utilizing all of my psychic senses, and I recognize these are gifts that are available to me always."

Then, take a deep breath, ask if there's anything else you need to learn from this particular lifetime, and open your eyes. Immediately record everything you experienced. Write down where you placed the rocks in relation to each psychic sense.

Your psychic senses are there for the taking, ready and willing to be employed throughout your life, in different ways, every day. It is up to you to grasp them and work with them. Psychic senses are your birthright—don't miss out!

Now, enjoy! You are an intuitive being!

bibliography

Brady, Teresa. *Ignite Your Psychic Intuition: An A to Z Guide to Developing Your Sixth Sense*. Woodbury, MN: Llewellyn Publications, 2011.

Chauran, Alexandra. *Crystal Ball Reading for Beginners: Easy Divination & Interpretation*. Woodbury, MN: Llewellyn Publications, 2011.

Chestney, Kim. *The Psychic Workshop: A Complete Program for Fulfilling Your Spiritual Potential*. Avon, MA: Adams Media, 2004.

Choquette, Sonia. *Trust Your Vibes: Secret Tools for Six-Sensory Living*. Carlsbad, CA: Hay House, 2004.

Coffey, Chip. *Growing Up Psychic: My Story of Not Just Surviving but Thriving … And How Others Like Me Can, Too.* New York: Crown Publishing Group, 2012.

Cunningham, Scott. *Divination for Beginners: Read the Past, Present & Future.* Woodbury, MN: Llewellyn Publications, 2003.

Hewitt, William W. *Psychic Development for Beginners: An Easy Guide to Releasing and Developing Your Psychic Abilities.* Woodbury, MN: Llewellyn Publications, 1996.

Howard, Vernon. *A Treasury of Trueness: Gems of Wisdom.* Pine, AZ: New Life Foundation, 1995.

Kenner, Corrine. *Crystals for Beginners: A Guide to Collecting & Using Stones & Crystals.* Woodbury, MN: Llewellyn Publications, 2006.

Martin, Barbara Y. and Dimitri Moraitis. *The Healing Power of Your Aura: How to Use Spiritual Energy for Physical Health and Well-Being.* Sunland, CA: Spiritual Arts Institute, 2006.

McCoy, Edain. *How to Do Automatic Writing.* St. Paul, MN: Llewellyn Publications, 1994.

Mishlove, Jeffrey. *The PK Man: A True Story of Mind Over Matter.* Charlottesville, VA: Hampton Roads Publishing Company, 2000.

Peirce, Penney. *Frequency: The Power of Personal Vibration.* New York: Atria, Simon & Schuster, 2009.

"Uri Geller's Short Biography," accessed April 16, 2014, http://site.uri-geller.com/en/uri_geller_s_short_biography.

VanZant, Iyanla. *The Value in the Valley: A Black Woman's Guide Through Life's Dilemmas.* New York: Fireside, Simon & Schuster, 1995.

Webster, Richard. *Pendulum Magic for Beginners: Tap Into Your Inner Wisdom.* Woodbury, MN: Llewellyn Publications, 2002.

Weiss, Brian L. *Many Lives, Many Masters: The True Story of a Prominent Psychiatrist, His Young Patient, and the Past-Life Therapy That Changed Both Their Lives.* New York: Fireside, Simon & Schuster, 1988.

———. *Miracles Happen: The Transformational Healing Power of Past-Life Memories.* New York: HarperCollins Publishers, 2012.

Zantamata, Doe. Karma: *Happiness in Your Life: Book 1 of 12.* Iko Productions, 2012.

suggested reading

Alvarez, Melissa. *365 Ways to Raise Your Frequency: Simple Tools to Increase Your Spiritual Energy for Balance, Purpose, and Joy.* Woodbury, MN: Llewellyn Publications, 2012.

Harper, Elizabeth. *Wishing: How to Fulfill Your Heart's Desires.* New York: Atria Books, Simon & Schuster, 2008.

Robinett, Kristy. *Messenger Between Worlds: True Stories from a Psychic Medium.* Woodbury, MN: Llewellyn Publications, 2013.

To Write to the Author

If you wish to contact the author or would like more information about this book, please write to the author in care of Llewellyn Worldwide Ltd., and we will forward your request. Both the author and publisher appreciate hearing from you and learning of your enjoyment of this book and how it has helped you. Llewellyn Worldwide Ltd. cannot guarantee that every letter written to the author can be answered, but all will be forwarded. Please write to:

Melanie Barnum
℅ Llewellyn Worldwide
2143 Wooddale Drive
Woodbury, MN 55125-2989

Please enclose a self-addressed stamped envelope for reply, or $1.00 to cover costs. If outside the USA, enclose an international postal reply coupon.

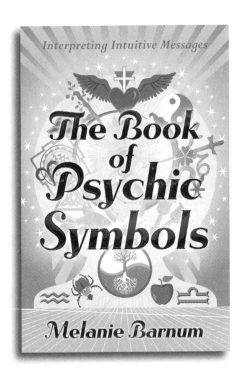

Interpreting Intuitive Messages

The Book
of
Psychic
Symbols

Melanie Barnum

The Book of Psychic Symbols
Interpreting Intuitive Messages
Melanie Barnum

A strong feeling, a remarkable coincidence, a strange dream ... What may seem ordinary could actually be an important message—a helpful hint or a warning from a deceased loved one or spirit guide. Open yourself to a wealth of guidance and opportunities by learning how to recognize and interpret the signs and synchronicities all around us.

The Book of Psychic Symbols can help you decode dreams, intuitive flashes, and all psychic impressions. Intuitive counselor Melanie Barnum explains what psychic symbols are, how we receive them, and where they come from. She also shares amazing stories from her life that clarify how the wondrous intuitive process works. In addition to a comprehensive dictionary of 500 symbols, there are many practical exercises for exploring symbols in your life, fortifying your natural intuition, and using psychic symbols to manifest your desires.

978-0-7387-2303-7, 288 pp., 6 x 9   **$15.95**

The
Steady
Way to
Greatness

Liberate Your Intuitive Potential
& Manifest Your Heartfelt Desires

MELANIE BARNUM

The Steady Way to Greatness
Liberate Your Intuitive Potential
& Manifest Your Heartfelt Desires
Melanie Barnum

Use intuition and psychic development to master the law of attraction and manifest the life you truly desire. The Steady Way to Greatness is a new and groundbreaking combination of manifestation and intuition for success in career, finances, love, relationships, spirituality, and more. Organized into a progression of fifty-two weekly practices, this guide includes affirmations and other exercises designed to increase confidence, discover the power of goal setting, and expose the magnificence that resides within.

Intuitive counselor Melanie Barnum is the perfect guide to help you reach your true potential. The stories and exercises she includes are designed for:

- Exploring positive and negative attitudes
- Opening to intuitive senses
- Identifying strengths
- Creating and living your dream life

978-0-7387-3835-2, 264 pp., 6 x 9   **$15.99**

Over 150,000 Sold!

Psychic Development

For Beginners

An Easy Guide to Developing and Releasing
Your Psychic Abilities

WILLIAM W. HEWITT

Psychic Development for Beginners
An Easy Guide to Developing and Releasing Your Psychic Abilities
WILLIAM W. HEWITT

MORE THAN 150,000 SOLD!

You possess a secret power that is just waiting to be harnessed—your natural psychic sense.

This unique book on psychic development offers fast and easy techniques that can be used every day to solve problems, psychically shield yourself from harm, contact your spirit guide, attain superior listening skills, boost your reading comprehension, and even reserve that perfect parking space in advance.

Awaken and develop your innate psychic abilities, and ultimately create the kind of life you have always dreamed of. More than 44 fun and simple activities and 28 case studies in this book on psychic development illustrate the effectiveness of these methods.

978-1-56718-360-3, 216 pp., 5¼ x 8   **$14.99**

So You Want to Be a PSYCHIC INTUITIVE?

A Down-to-Earth Guide

Alexandra Chauran

So You Want to Be a Psychic Intuitive?
A Down-to-Earth Guide
ALEXANDRA CHAURAN

Dependable guidance, communication with departed loved ones, helping friends and family—the lifelong rewards of a strong psychic connection are countless. Whether you're a beginner or already in touch with your intuition, this encouraging, conversational, and hands-on guide can help you improve psychic abilities. Featuring illustrative anecdotes and easy exercises, you'll learn how to achieve a receptive state, identify your source of information, receive messages, and interpret coincidences, dreams, and symbols. Step-by-step instructions make it easy to try a variety of psychic techniques and divination, such as telepathy, channeling, spirit communication, automatic writing, and scrying. There's also practical advice for wisely applying your enhanced psychic skills personally and professionally.

978-0-7387-3065-3, 264 pp, 5³/₁₆ x 8   **$14.95**